IN THE
WORDS OF
OUR
ENEMIES

IN THE WORDS OF OUR ENEMIES

JED BABBIN

Since 1947
REGNERY
PUBLISHING, INC.
An Eagle Publishing Company • Washington, DC

Library of Congress Cataloging-in-Publication Data

Babbin, Jed L.
  In the words of our enemies / Jed Babbin.
      p. cm.
  Includes bibliographical references and index.
  ISBN 978-1-59698-523-0
  1. War on Terrorism, 2001–2. United States–Foreign rela-
tions–2001–3. Terrorism–Government policy–United States. I. Title.
  HV6432.B32 2007
  327.73—dc22

                                            2007019512

Published in the United States by
Regnery Publishing, Inc.
One Massachusetts Avenue, NW
Washington, DC 20001

www.regnery.com
Manufactured in the United States of America

10 9 8 7 6 5 4 3 2 1

Books are available in quantity for promotional or premium use. Write to Director of Special Sales, Regnery Publishing, Inc., One Massachusetts Avenue NW, Washington, DC 20001, for information on discounts and terms or call (202) 216-0600.

To those who strive not just to see but to observe,
who not only hear, but listen and exert themselves to understand,
to those who have the courage to judge and not merely accept,
and especially to my father who taught me how to do it
and why it must be done

HAROLD H. BABBIN
Captain, USMCR (1917–1978)

Contents

Foreword

BY NEWT GINGRICH

The Associated Press reported in March of 2007 that terrorists in Iraq had passed an unthinkable threshold: They used two children to disguise a car bomb. The car was waved through a checkpoint by American soldiers who could not imagine that children would be in a car filled with explosives. When the terrorists got to their target, they got out of the car and ran. They left the children behind in the car, and then blew it up.

There is a word for people who put children in a car to be blown up. The word is evil.

When I travel around the country speaking to groups of Americans, I often tell the story of a couple arrested last year in Great Britain. They were arrested on the suspicion that they were going to use their eight-month-old baby to smuggle a bomb onto an airplane. They were apparently going to disguise the bomb as baby food. And they were perfectly happy to kill their baby just as long as they killed some Americans in the process.

There is a word for people like this. The word is evil.

It's important that we say this out loud and that we render this moral judgment. Because if we fail to understand that our enemy is evil, we have failed to understand what we are fighting.

We are not used to adversaries who will kill young children—even their own children—just to get a chance to kill us. But we had better get used to it, because this is the level of seriousness in the threat we face—this is the level of its ferocity. And yet I wonder if some of us are still not prepared to recognize and confront the evil of our enemies.

America's liberal elite seem to be literally afraid to face the fact that we are at war. I think of their reaction when Khalid Sheik Mohammed, the leading captured terrorist from al Qaeda, offered a startling confession. He was almost certainly embellishing what he had done, but still, he told a chilling tale. He spoke unapologetically of the terrorist acts he had committed and those he had wished to commit.

He took responsibility for killing almost three thousand people on September 11, 2001. He said he had cut off a reporter's head, held it in his hand, and had his picture taken with it. And what was the reaction of two United States senators? They were worried that we had mistreated Khalid Sheik Mohammed in captivity.

They didn't walk out of the room and say this is a frightening example of how serious our enemies are. They worried that we were dealing incorrectly with the man who had just finished saying how much he wanted to slaughter us. This is a suicidal inability to come to grips with evil.

It reminds me of something the great historian William Manchester once said of the elites in the years leading up to World War II. It was the spring of 1939, after the Munich agreement had failed, after Hitler had absorbed the rest of Czechoslovakia, and after it was obvious that all the deals the democracies had made with Nazi Germany—all the appeasement—had failed. As Europe moved toward war, Winston Churchill tried to create a Ministry of Supply in Great Britain for the terrible war he knew was coming.

The public supported him and even the newspapers supported him. But the people Manchester called "the men of Munich"—the elite, those who could not bring themselves to believe that Hitler was evil, that he meant what he said—blocked Churchill at every turn. They would rather risk defeat than admit that they had been wrong.

Today, we have the Men and Women of Munich. Just as before, these are elites who are afraid to face evil, afraid to recognize what our enemies are doing, and afraid to put partisanship aside and put America first so we can join together to defeat those who would destroy us.

The Men and Women of Munich considered it a victory in Congress when they passed a bill that they had enthusiastically told their left-wing allies was designed to end the war in Iraq by crippling our military's ability to achieve victory.

Think about what that means. They didn't stand up courageously to vote to cut off funding for the war and take responsibility. No, they avoided responsibility and sent the president a bill designed to fail and leave young Americans in uniform to pay the price.

This inability to recognize the evil of our enemy isn't just in our government. Remember the story about the terrorists who used two children to disguise a car bomb in Iraq? Do you know how the editors at the Associated Press chose to headline that story? Not "Terrorists Slaughter Children, Save Themselves." Incredibly, the headline was "U.S. Destroys Bomb Factory in Iraq."

Talk about burying the lead.

Another news report surfaced recently that again displayed how Western society is failing to confront the true nature of our enemies because of the insane demands of political correctness.

In Germany, a Moroccan-born German woman filed for divorce because her husband regularly beat her and had threatened to kill her. She had police reports to back her up. But the judge refused to grant a divorce on the grounds that the Koran allows husbands to beat their wives. In other words, the judge set aside the German constitution in favor of "respecting" religious fanaticism. As for what it means for the future of Germany—and Western civilization for that matter—one German elected official put it best: "When the Koran takes precedence over basic German law, then I can only say: 'Goodnight, Germany.'"

We are living in serious times—a time when all of us need to think of the needs of our country and its future rather than our own personal or party interest. And despite the somber tone of my message, I'm hopeful about our future. In the years before World War II, the people of Great Britain and America eventually saw what the elites refused to see. They saw their futures, their families' futures, and the great civilization they had built threatened. And so they acted to defend them.

Many Americans have this same understanding today; they're not interested in the cheap political points that consume politicians in Washington; they're not blinded by political correctness. But they are demanding that their families and our nation be defended. They are demanding something more serious and more substantive from their leaders. And I have a feeling they're going to get it—that American leadership will again rise to the occasion of the crisis.

And if you think we're not in a crisis, the following record of what our enemies are saying about us should change your mind. Jed Babbin has compiled an invaluable record of what America's enemies, from Osama bin Laden to Hugo Chavez to the radical regimes of North Korea and Iran, are saying about their intentions towards us. We've been warned. It's up to us now to make sure we have the leaders necessary to mount America's defense.

Adapted from Newt Gingrich's Winning the Future newsletter.
For more information, visit www.winningthefuture.org.

To distinguish between the sun and the moon is no test of vision; to hear the thunderclap is no indication of acute hearing.

—Sun Tzu, The Art of War, c. 400–320 B.C.

Introduction

"It is difficult to find a parallel to the unwisdom of the British and weakness of the French Governments in this disastrous period. Nor can the United States escape the censure of history. Absorbed in their own affairs and all the abounding interests, activities and accidents of a free community, they simply gaped at the vast changes which were taking place in Europe, and imagined they were no concern of theirs. The considerable corps of highly competent, widely trained American professional officers formed their own opinions, but these produced no noticeable effect upon the improvident aloofness of American foreign policy. If the influence of the United States had been exerted, it might have galvanized the French and British politicians into action. The League of Nations, battered though it had been, was still an august instrument which would have invested any challenge to the new Hitler war menace with the sanctions of international law. Under the strain the Americans merely shrugged their shoulders, so that in a few years they had to pour out the blood and treasures of the New World to save themselves from mortal danger."

—WINSTON CHURCHILL[1]

Churchill wrote and spoke much of World War II, but one conclusion he reached about that war should be on every American's mind today: "There never was a war in all history easier to prevent by timely action." Few of us are his equal, but we all must seek to understand and apply the lessons he sought to teach. What wars can we prevent? And if they cannot be prevented, how can we better position our nation to win? Perhaps we should listen to our enemies.

We Americans are great talkers, but are often not great listeners. And what we do hear, we often mistake, because we tend to see our adversaries as people of the same mind as ourselves. When some dictator threatens to end our way of life, destroy our economy, or end our influence over his nation, we usually either ignore him or rationalize his statements in our own context rather than judge him better through an understanding of his culture, history, and ideology. He can't be evil, can he? He and his people will only act in their enlightened self-interest, won't they? But he can be, and they may not.

This book is not a call to war or even a war warning. The superfluity of the latter is evidenced by the many conflicts in which we are engaged, both military and geopolitical. It is, instead, a call to listen, to study, to understand in the context of the complex world in which we live the plain words that our enemies and potential enemies say to us and to each other. It is a reminder to be vigilant. It is, I hope, a searchlight we can use to penetrate the forest of events that surrounds us and find the narrow paths around the wars that may—like the war against terrorists and the nations that support them—come upon us unaware.

For us to understand the challenges our nation faces, we must filter the danger out of the noise. It is easy, and cheap, for any person, political party, or nation to condemn or threaten America. There is no penalty for taking the floor of the UN General

Assembly or touring the capitals of Europe to denounce America's influence in the world. To the contrary, those who do are usually acclaimed in the media and feted in places such as Beijing and Moscow, Tehran and Caracas. Most of this is posturing, but some is assuredly not. Those that are not portend dangers near and far. In this work, I begin the filtering process, separating the serious—the Osama bin Ladens and Vladimir Putins of the world—from the nuisances such as Zimbabwe's Robert Mugabe and the other despots, dictators, and rogues who comprise the majority of the UN General Assembly. Consider this: of the 192 members of the UN, fewer than half—a generous count yields a total of ninety nations—are "free," and the rest deny their citizens the rights we take for granted and which are guaranteed under our Constitution.

There are three admonitions for you, the reader.

First, the following chapters are not comprehensive. Nations and their leaders can rise from nuisance to danger and then fade back into the noise. Libya's Muammar Qaddafi has made that transformation more than once, and may again. Also, adversaries are not all as obvious as those catalogued here, and there will inevitably be some I have failed to illuminate.

Second, many of our adversaries make alliances of convenience both in the open and in secret, both temporarily and longer-term. As dangerous as any nation or terrorist group may be alone, such alliances often make the resulting threat more dangerous than the mere sum of the parts. In turn, alliances we may make—brief or sustained—can analogously reduce those threats. The world has many moving parts. Just because America is preoccupied with one or two does not mean we can afford to ignore the dozens of others that may prove more important.

Third, most of what you will read here was published openly in languages other than English, the speaker or writer confident that it would not be revealed to those unable to understand the speaker's tongue. Remember that throughout his murderous career, Yasser Arafat preached peace in English while exhorting his followers to violence in Arabic. We were unable to find his constant refrain—"To Jerusalem we are going as martyrs in the millions"—ever stated in English. Most of what you will read here was not meant for your eyes.

Many of the passages set forth here are long by American standards. Fidel Castro and Hugo Chavez aren't the only egotists who give speeches that go on for hours. Many of the speeches, "religious" judgments (fatwas), and sermons you shall read are very long because in Islamist terms, the call to kill must not be stated in purely political, warlike terms. The radical Islamists must convincingly cloak themselves in the religious righteousness of their cause, and derive from their own interpretations of religious law the necessity to commit the vicious murders they champion. It takes a long speech to sew all of that together, to make it convincing to the followers who are being ordered to commit suicide, to kill, and thus achieve Heaven.

These words are important because they have meaning and consequences. We must listen and absorb. Study and analyze. Assemble the scattered parts and think. Judge for ourselves. Our nation is enormously strong—militarily, politically, economically, and even diplomatically—but as September 11, 2001, proved, our great strengths are no guarantee of safety. Is the poor performance of our intelligence community the only explanation? Or did we just not listen to the clear words of our enemy?

ONE

Before September 11

Five years before September 11, Osama bin Laden had made clear his intentions to strike the United States by any and every means. But like Hitler in 1924, bin Laden wasn't yet a credible threat. He had declared himself our enemy and announced clearly that he wanted to drive America out of Saudi Arabia, where Mecca and Medina, the holiest places in Islam, are located. More important, he explained why he believed his Islamofascists could defeat America: every time we had been attacked by terrorists, we had retreated.

The terrorist ideology bin Laden shares with Hizballah, Hamas, and so many others is Nietzschean: they believe what does not annihilate their followers completely makes those still alive stronger, and will cause many more adherents to join their cause. Bin Laden's 1996 fatwa cites every incident, beginning with the Reagan administration's withdrawal from Lebanon after the Marine barracks bombing in 1983, as proof of American weakness. The following is from bin Laden's August 1996 fatwa against America, first published in the London newspaper Al-Quds Al-Arabi:[1]

[A f]ew days ago the news agencies had reported that the defense secretary of the Crusading Americans had said that "the explosion at Riyadh and Al-Khobar had taught him one lesson: that is not to withdraw when attacked by coward terrorists."

We say to the defense secretary that his talk can induce a grieving mother to laughter! and shows the fears that had enshrined you all. Where was this false courage of yours when the explosion in Beirut took place on 1983 AD (1403 A.H). You were turned into scattered [b]its and pieces at that time; 241 mainly marine solders were killed. And where was this courage of yours when two explosions made you . . . leave Aden in less than twenty-four hours!

But your most disgraceful case was in Somalia, where—after vigorous propaganda about the power of the USA and its post–cold war leadership of the new world order—you moved tens of thousands of international force[s], including twenty-eight thousand American soldiers, into Somalia. However, when . . . [many] of your soldiers were killed in minor battles and one American pilot was dragged in the streets of Mogadishu, you left the area carrying disappointment, humiliation, defeat, and your dead with you. Clinton appeared in front of the whole world threatening and promising revenge, but these threats were merely a preparation for withdrawal. You have been disgraced by Allah and you withdrew; the extent of your impotence and weaknesses became very clear. It was a pleasure for the "heart" of every Muslim and a remedy to the "chests" of believing nations to see you defeated in the three Islamic cities of Beirut, Aden, and Mogadishu.

I say to you, [Clinton] Secretary of Defense [William Cohen]: The sons of the land of the two Holy Places had come out to fight against the Russian[s] in Afghanistan, the Serb[s] in Bosnia-Herzegovina and today they are fighting in Chechnya and, by the Permission of Allah, they have been made victorious over your partner, the Russians. By the command of Allah, they are also fighting in Tajikistan.

I say: Since the sons of the land of the two Holy Places feel and strongly believe that fighting (Jihad) against the Kuffar in every part of the world, is absolutely essential; then they would be even more enthusiastic, more powerful and larger in number upon fighting on their own land—the place of their births—defending the greatest of their sanctities, the noble Ka'ba (the Qiblah of all Muslims). They know that the Muslims of the world will assist and help them to victory. To liberate their sanctities is the greatest of issues concerning all Muslims; it is the duty of every Muslim in this world.

I say to you, William [Cohen], that **these youths love death as you love life**. They inherit dignity, pride, courage, generosity, truthfulness, and sacrifice from father to father. They are most delivering and steadfast at war. They inherit these values from their ancestors (even from the time of the Jaheliyyah, before Islam). These values were approved and completed by the arriving Islam as stated by the messenger of Allah (Allah's Blessings and Salutations may be on him): "I have been sen[t] to [teach] . . . good values." (Saheeh Al-Jame' As-Sagheer).

When the pagan King Amroo Ibn Hind tried to humiliate the pagan Amroo Ibn Kulthoom, the latter cut the head of the king with his sword rejecting aggression, humiliation, and indignation.

If the king oppresses the people excessively, we reject submitting to humiliation.

By which legitimacy (or command) O Amroo bin Hind you want us to be degraded?!

By which legitimacy (or command) O Amroo bin Hind you listen to our foes and disrespect us?!

Our toughness has, O Amroo, tired the enemies before you, never giving in!

Our youths believe in paradise after death. They believe that taking part in fighting will not bring their day nearer; and staying behind will not postpone their day either. Exalted be to Allah who said: 'And a soul will not die but with the permission of Allah.'

Our youths took note of the meaning of the poetic verse: "If death is a predetermined must, then it is a shame to die cowardly," and the other poet saying: "Who do[es] not die by the sword will die by other reason; many causes are there but one death."

These youths believe in what has been told by Allah and His messenger (Allah's Blessings and Salutations may be on him) about the greatness of the reward for the Mujahideen and Martyrs; Allah, the most exalted said: "...those who are slain in the way of Allah, He will by no means allow their deeds to perish. He will guide them and improve their condition, and cause them to enter the garden...which He has made known to them." (Muhammad; 47:4–6). Allah the Exalted also said: "...do not speak of those who are slain in Allah's way as dead...they are alive, but you do not perceive" (Bagarah; 2:154).

His messenger (Allah's Blessings and Salutations may be on him) said: "for those who strive in His cause Allah prepared hundred degrees (levels) in paradise; in between two degrees as in between heaven and earth." Saheeh Al-Jame' As-Sagheer. He (Allah's Blessings and Salutations may be on him) also said: "the best of the martyrs are those who do NOT turn their faces away from the battle [until] they are killed. They are in the high level of Jannah (paradise). Their Lord laughs to them (in pleasure) and when your Lord laughs to a slave of His, He will not hold him to an account...a martyr will not feel the pain of death except like how you feel when you are pinched." Saheeh Al-Jame' As-Sagheer, he also said: "a martyr privileges are guaranteed by Allah; forgiveness with the first gush of his blood, he will be shown his seat in paradise, he will be decorated with the jewels of belief (Imaan), married off to the beautiful ones, protected from the test in the grave, assured security in the day of judgement, crowned with the crown of dignity, a ruby of which is better than this whole world (Duniah) and its entire content, wedded to seventy-two of the pure Houries (beautiful ones of Paradise) and his intercession on the behalf of seventy of his relatives will be accepted." Narrated by Ahmad and At-Tirmithi (with the correct and trustworthy reference).

Those youths know that their rewards in fighting you, the USA, is double than their rewards in fighting someone else not from the people of the book. **They have no intention except to enter paradise by killing you.** An infidel, and enemy of God like you, cannot be in the same hell with his righteous executioner.

Our youths chanting and reciting the word of Allah, the most exalted: "fight them; Allah will punish them by your hands and bring them to disgrace, and assist you against them and heal the heart of a believing people..."

The youths also reciting the All Mighty words of: "so when you me[e]t in battle those who disbelieve, then smite the necks...." (Muhammad; 47:19). Those youths will not ask you (William Cohen) for explanations; they will tell you singing [that] there is nothing between us [that] need[s] to be explained, there is only killing and neck-smiting.

And they will say to you what their grandfather, Haroon Ar-Rasheed, Ameer-ul-Mu'meneen, replied to your grandfather, Nagfoor, the Byzantine emperor, when he threatened the Muslims: "from Haroon Ar-Rasheed, Ameer-ul-Mu'meneen, to Nagfoor, the dog of the Romans; the answer is what you will see not what you hear." Haroon Ar-Rasheed led the armies of Islam to the battle and handed Nagfoor a devastating defeat.

The youths you called cowards are competing among themselves for fighting and killing you. Reciting what one of them said: "The crusader army became dust when we detonated al-Khobar." With courageous youth of Islam fearing no danger. If (they are) threatened: The tyrants will kill you, they reply, "my death is a victory. I did not betray that king, he did betray our Qiblah. And he permitted in the holy country the most filthy sort of humans. I have made an oath by Allah, the Great, to fight whoever rejected the faith." For more than a decade, they carried arms on their shoulders in Afghanistan and they have made vows to Allah that as long as they are alive, they will continue to carry arms against you until you are—Allah willing—expelled, defeated and humiliated, they will carry on as long as they live. . . .

By the time bin Laden issued that statement, he had already taken actions, through al Qaeda and the network of Islamic terrorist groups with which it was allied, to kill Americans. In October 1993, in Mogadishu, Somalia, al Qaeda helped the forces of warlord Mohamed Aideed shoot down an American helicopter in the incident portrayed in the movie Black Hawk Down, in which eighteen Americans were killed. The world witnessed Aideed's barbarians dragging the torn body of helicopter crew chief Bill Cleveland through the streets of Mogadishu. We should have known more *about bin Laden's claims that he was involved in the inhuman acts we witnessed on television, but few—even inside our government— paid much attention to his words.*

Though the public knew little about bin Laden, we could have learned more if we had paid attention to his public words. In March 1997, months after al Qaeda killed more than a dozen Americans in the attack on the Khobar Towers barracks in Saudi Arabia, Peter Arnett of CNN brought bin Laden into our living rooms. This interview gave us insight into bin Laden's terrorist "Newspeak." His mind works much as Hitler's did, establishing "rights" to commit terrorist acts to avenge the "injustice" America brings to the Middle East. Bin Laden boasts of his victory in Mogadishu and states plainly his intent. The interview was conducted in Afghanistan:

REPORTER: Now, the United States government says that you are still funding military training camps here in Afghanistan for militant Islamic fighters and that you are a sponsor of international terrorism; but others describe you as the new hero of the Arab-Islamic world. Are these accusations true? How do you describe yourself?

BIN LADEN: After the collapse of the Soviet Union—in which the U.S. ha[d] no mentionable role, but rather the credit goes to God, Praise and Glory be to Him, and the Mujahidin in Afghanistan— this collapse made the U.S. more haughty and arrogant and it has started to look at itself as a master of this world and established what it calls the new world order. It wanted to delude people that it can do whatever it wants, but it can't do this. It leveled against me and others as many accusations as it desired and wished. It is these (accusations) that you mentioned.

The U.S. today as a result of the arrogant atmosphere has set a double standard, calling whoever goes against its injustice a terrorist. It wants to occupy our countries, steal our resources, impose on us agents to rule us based not on what God has revealed and wants us to agree on all these. If we refuse to do so, it will say you are terrorists. With a simple look at the U.S. behaviors, we find that it judges the behavior of the poor Palestinian children whose country was occupied: if they throw stones against the Israeli occupation, it says they are terrorists whereas when the Israeli pilots bombed the United Nations building in Qana, Lebanon was full of children and women, the U.S. stopped any plan to condemn Israel.

At the time that they condemn any Muslim who calls for his right, they receive the highest top official of the Irish Republican Army (Gerry Adams) at the White House as a political leader, while woe, all woe is the Muslims if they cry out for their rights. Wherever we look, we find the U.S. as the leader of terrorism and crime in the world. The U.S. does not consider it a terrorist act to throw atomic bombs at nations thousands of miles away, when it would not be possible for those bombs to hit military troops only. These bombs were rather thrown at entire nations, including women, children, and elderly people and up to this day the traces of those bombs remain in Japan. The U.S. does not consider it terrorism when hundreds of thousands of our sons and brothers in Iraq died for lack of food or medicine.

So, there is no base for what the U.S. says and this saying does not affect us, because we, by the grace of God, are dependent on Him, Praise and Glory be to Him, getting help from Him against the U.S. As for the last part of your question, we are fulfilling a duty which God, Praise and Glory be to Him, decreed for us. We look upon those heroes, those men who undertook to kill the American occupiers in Riyadh and Khobar (Dhahran). We describe those as heroes and describe them as men. They have pulled down the disgrace and submissiveness off the forehead of their nation. We ask Allah, Praise and Glory be to Him, to accept them as martyrs.

REPORTER: Let's go to the bombings of United States troops in Riyadh and Dhahran. Why did they happen and were you and your supporters involved in these attacks?

BIN LADEN: As for the previous question, the explosion of Riyadh and the one in Al-Khobar (Dhahran), it is no secret that during the two explosions, I was not in Saudi Arabia, but I have great respect for the people who did this action. I say, as I said before, they are heroes. We look upon them as men who wanted to raise the flag of "there is no God but Allah," and to put an end to the non-believers and the state of injustice that the U.S. brought. I also say that what they did is a great job and a big honor that I missed participating in.[2]

A year later, on February 23, 1998, bin Laden issued another fatwa against Americans. It said, in part:

The Arabian Peninsula has never—since Allah made it flat, created its desert, and encircled it with seas—been stormed by any forces like the crusader armies spreading in it like locusts, eating its riches and wiping out its plantations. All this is happening at a time in which nations are attacking Muslims like people fighting over a plate of food. In the light of the grave situation and the lack of support, we and you are obliged to discuss current events, and we should all agree on how to settle the matter.

No one argues today about three facts that are known to everyone; we will list them, in order to remind everyone:

First, for over seven years, the United States has been occupying the lands of Islam in the holiest of places, the Arabian Peninsula, plundering its riches, dictating to its rulers, humiliating its people, terrorizing its neighbors, and turning its bases in the Peninsula into a spearhead through which to fight the neighboring Muslim peoples.

If some people have in the past argued about the fact of the occupation, all the people of the peninsula have now acknowledged it. The best proof of this is the Americans' continuing aggression against the Iraqi people using the peninsula as a staging post, even though all its rulers are against their territories being used to that end, but they are helpless.

Second, despite the great devastation inflicted on the Iraqi people by the crusader-Zionist alliance, and despite the huge number of those killed, which has exceeded one million... despite all this, the Americans are once again trying to repeat the horrific massacres, as though they are not content with the protracted blockade imposed after the ferocious war or the fragmentation and devastation.

So here they come to annihilate what is left of this people and to humiliate their Muslim neighbors.

Third, if the Americans' aims behind these wars are religious and economic, the aim is also to serve the Jews' petty state and divert attention from its occupation of Jerusalem and murder of Muslims there. The best proof of this is their eagerness to destroy Iraq, the strongest neighboring Arab state, and their endeavor to fragment all the states of the region such as Iraq, Saudi Arabia, Egypt, and Sudan into paper statelets and through their disunion and weakness to guarantee Israel's survival and the continuation of the brutal crusade occupation of the Peninsula.

All these crimes and sins committed by the Americans are a clear declaration of war on Allah, his messenger, and Muslims. And ulema have throughout Islamic history unanimously agreed that the jihad is an individual duty if the enemy destroys the Muslim countries. This was revealed by Imam Bin-Qadamah in "Al-Mughni," Imam al-Kisa'i in "Al-Bada'i," al-Qurtubi in his interpretation, and the shaykh of al-Islam in his books, where he said: "As for the fighting to repulse [an enemy], it is aimed at defending sanctity and religion, and it is a duty as agreed [by the ulema]. Nothing is more sacred than belief except repulsing an enemy who is attacking religion and life."

On that basis, and in compliance with Allah's order, we issue the following fatwa to all Muslims:

The ruling to kill the Americans and their allies—civilians and military—is an individual duty for every Muslim who can do it in any country in which it is possible to do it, in order to liberate the al-Aqsa Mosque and the holy mosque [Mecca] from their grip, and in order for their armies to move out of all the lands of Islam, defeated and unable to threaten any Muslim. This is in accordance with the words of Almighty Allah, "and fight the pagans all together as they fight you all together," and "fight them until there is no more tumult or oppression, and there prevail justice and faith in Allah."

By then bin Laden and al Qaeda had risen high above the noise level. They were powerful actors on the world's stage, responsible for the deaths of many Americans. But still we didn't listen. In May

1998, about two months before al Qaeda bombed two American embassies in Africa, ABC's John Miller interviewed bin Laden at his camp in southern Afghanistan. Again, the enemy told us—clearly— that terrorism was his legal right and there was an obligation to abolish what he and his followers believe to be American terrorism against Muslims:

BIN LADEN: There is an Arabic proverb that says "she accused me of having her malady, then snuck away." Besides, terrorism can be commendable and it can be reprehensible. Terrifying an innocent person and terrorizing him is objectionable and unjust, also unjustly terrorizing people is not right. Whereas, terrorizing oppressors and criminals and thieves and robbers is necessary for the safety of people and for the protection of their property. There is no doubt in this. Every state and every civilization and culture has to resort to terrorism under certain circumstances for the pur-pose of abolishing tyranny and corruption. Every country in the world has its own security system and its own security forces, its own police and its own army. They are all designed to terrorize whoever even contemplates to attack that country or its citizens. The terrorism we practice is of the commendable kind for it is directed at the tyrants and the aggressors and the enemies of Allah, the tyrants, the traitors who commit acts of treason against their own countries and their own faith and their own prophet and their own nation. Terrorizing those and punishing them are nec-essary measures to straighten things and to make them right. Tyrants and oppressors who subject the Arab nation to aggression ought to be punished.

The Western regimes and the government of the United States of America bear the blame for what might happen. If their people do not wish to be harmed inside their very own countries, they should seek to elect governments that are truly representative of them and that can protect their interests.

Tell the Muslims everywhere that the vanguards of the warriors who are fighting the enemies of Islam belong to them and the young fighters are their sons. Tell them that the nation is bent on fighting the enemies of Islam. Once again, I have to stress the necessity of focusing on the Americans and the Jews, for they represent the spearhead with which the members of our religion have been slaughtered. Any effort directed against America and the Jews yields positive and direct results—Allah willing. **It is far better for anyone to kill a single American soldier than to squander his effort on other activities**.... [3]

We believe that the worst thieves in the world today and the worst terrorists are the Americans. Nothing could stop you except perhaps retaliation in kind. **We do not have to differentiate between military or civilian. As far as we are concerned, they are all targets**, and this is what the fatwah says.... The fatwah is general (comprehensive) and **it includes all those who participate in, or help the Jewish occupiers in killing Muslims**....

We are certain—with the grace of Allah—that we shall prevail over the Jews and over those fighting with them. Today however, our battle against the Americans is far greater than our battle was against the Russians. Americans have committed unprecedented stupidity. They have attacked Islam and its most significant sacrosanct symbols.... **We anticipate a black future for America. Instead of remaining united states, it shall end up separated states and shall have to carry the bodies of its sons back to America**....

JOHN MILLER: Describe the situation when your men took down the American forces in Somalia.

BIN LADEN: After our victory in Afghanistan and the defeat of the oppressors who had killed millions of Muslims, the legend about the invincibility of the superpowers vanished. Our boys no longer viewed America as a superpower. So, when they left Afghanistan, they went to Somalia and prepared themselves carefully for a long war. They had thought that the Americans were like the Russians, so they trained and prepared. **They were stunned when they discovered how low was the morale of the American soldier.** America had entered with 30,000 soldiers in addition to thousands of soldiers from different countries in the world. . . . As I said, our boys were shocked by the low morale of the American soldier and they realized that the American soldier was just a paper tiger. He was unable to endure the strikes that were dealt to his army, so he fled, and America had to stop all its bragging and all that noise it was making in the press. . . .

Six months after this interview—almost three years before September 11—on November 6, 1998, a New York federal grand jury returned an indictment against bin Laden charging him with organizing, training, and operating terrorist networks from Afghanistan to Sudan, smuggling weapons and explosives, and declaring terrorist war against the United States. We read news reports of the indictment and ignored its import. We were sufficiently blasé about his threat and arrogant in our own invulnerability that we contented ourselves that bin Laden was just a criminal to be hauled into court. It was inescapably clear, in 1998, that Osama bin Laden and his network were the enemy, and an enemy that was acting on its stated intentions. There was no doubt, three years before September 11, that bin Laden had risen above the noise level and was a threat that had to be dealt with before more Americans died. But we, the public, didn't demand action, and the Clinton administration—though it had reams of proof that the threat was both real and imminent— was incapable of doing anything more than attend the legal niceties.

Bin Laden was, in the minds of the Clinton administration, a law enforcement problem. Fortunately, those in the intelligence agencies and the Defense Department continued to push Bill Clinton to act. Tragically, he was personally disinterested and incapable of decisive action.

Even when Bill Clinton could no longer ignore the threat, and belatedly decided to take direct action against bin Laden, he still wouldn't act decisively. He dithered. It wasn't that America lacked the ability to defend itself; it lacked a leader who could act decisively to end a proven threat to American lives.

Even after the indictment, after the open recognition of bin Laden's abilities as a major threat in the 1998 indictment, we—the American public—still didn't listen to the enemy. We sat back while the Clinton administration achieved a historic level of fecklessness and waited. Bin Laden didn't turn to silence to continue his jihad against America. He was—at every turn—warning of what we should expect from him and his terrorist network.

Victimology Is the Heart of Islamofascism

At the heart of Islamofascism is victimology. Bin Laden, his allies, his enablers, and his apologists all use it as justification for terrorism against the West.

In his great study of Arab culture, The Arab Mind, Raphael Patai
examined at length the source of anti-Western hatred among the Arab
peoples. One of his conclusions summarizes the cultural-religious
basis for the terrorist ideology:

A very specific component was added to the Arab mind when
Western scholarship presented Arab literati with the historical
drama of medieval Arab greatness followed by centuries of stagnation. Arab critics soon outdistanced their Western colleagues in
chastising the Arabs for their backwardness, cultural decline,
indeed, fossilization. The thrust of these melancholy representations was always positive: they intended and actually managed to
awaken the Arab mind from its medieval slumber, implanted in it
the desire to recapture ancient glories and take its place alongside
the West in the cultural vanguard of humanity. Nationalism was
thought by many to be the panacea for all Arab ills, and Arab
nationalism contributed greatly to the liberation of the Arab
homeland from the Atlantic to the Persian Gulf.

At the same time Arab nationalism became tainted by a strong
anti-Western streak. While it had to be recognized that the West
was the prime mover in bringing about the Arab awakening, in
introducing sanitation, general education, and other mass benefits
into the Arab world, the West assumed for the Arab mind the character of a sinister jinni, a hateful enemy and a convenient whip-
ping-boy who could be blamed for all the problems that beset the
Arabs. The encounter with the West produced a disturbing inferiority complex in the Arab mind which in itself made it more difficult to shake off the shackles of stagnation. The next challenge the
Arab mind must meet is to cease measuring Arab achievements
with Western yardsticks and to work for a regeneration of the Arab
world by building on its own, by no means negligible, capabilities.[4]

Palestinian victimology has mired the Palestinians in the permanent role of cannon fodder for their Arab neighbors in an unending war against the existence of Israel. They are the only people of the world who seem incapable of acting in their own enlightened self-interest. For generations they have been willfully ignorant of the fact that their refusal to make peace with Israel serves only their enemies. Since Israel was created by UN mandate, the Palestinians have been rejected by Jordan (itself 60 percent Palestinian), Egypt, and Syria. Saudi Arabia and Lebanon don't want them. But for decades under Arafat, the Palestinians did the bidding of the same countries that rejected them. Syria, Egypt, Saudi Arabia, and others bought Arafat's regime for the price of terrorist campaigns against Israel. They fund and provide sanctuary for Hamas and other Palestinian terror groups for two reasons: first, to keep alive the Palestinians' hope of erasing Israel from the map; and second, to absorb the casualties in the terror war against Israel that those nations don't wish to suffer.

Bin Laden Continues the Buildup to September 11

Only two months after the indictment, Osama bin Laden was again on our doorsteps and in our mailboxes. Here's a quote from the January 11, 1999 issue of Time *magazine. Read it and think about his earlier vow to acquire weapons of mass destruction to use against us:*[5]

Hostility toward America is a religious duty, and we hope to be rewarded for it by God.... I am confident that Muslims will be able to end the legend of the so-called superpower that is America.

Acquiring weapons for the defense of Muslims is a religious duty. If I have indeed acquired these weapons, then I thank God for enabling me to do so. And if I seek to acquire these weapons,

I am carrying out a duty. It would be a sin for Muslims not to try to possess the weapons that would prevent the infidels from inflicting harm on Muslims.

For bin Laden, and every other terrorist, it is essential to gain publicity in order to claim credit for success, gather more money, and incent terrorists to flock to his cause. Bin Laden did so again, in a rare public appearance at the wedding of his son in southern Afghanistan in February 2001. Celebrating a wedding is, for the terrorists, just another opportunity to celebrate the deaths of Americans. Bin Laden said:

The pieces of the bodies of infidels were flying like dust particles. If you would have seen it with your own eyes, you would have been very pleased, and your heart would have been filled with joy.

That joy filled the hearts of Islamofascists—Iranians, Palestinians, the Taliban, Somalis and more—on September 11. It will, again and again, if we do not listen to them and to our other enemies.

The lessons of September 11 are mostly lost on us. We can blame the intelligence agencies for their obvious failures. The new Homeland Security bureaucracy seems to have learned little, for our borders are still open. But what have we, the public, learned?

The most important lesson for us is the one Churchill taught that we have yet to learn. If our enemies speak, we must take them seriously even if our government does not. Public opinion can drive our government to act. When the next September 11 happens, as it inevitably will, who shall we blame but ourselves?

TWO

The Hate Factories

Our Constitution's First Amendment provides that, "Congress shall make no law respecting the establishment of religion, or prohibiting the free exercise thereof. . . ." In a free society, a true democracy, the power of the state is divorced from religion. In nations based on the religious law of Islam, it is the precise opposite.

The Koran, Islam's holy writ, is vastly different from our Constitution. The Constitution sets out the limits of the state and the laws it may create to regulate the lives of citizens. The Koran not only prescribes the tenets of the religion, but it also states a comprehensive legal code by which Muslims are supposed to live. It regulates almost every aspect of Muslim life, from daily life and civil law to the tenets of war.

When an American congressman speaks, he speaks in the context of American law and policy, and no congressman or senator presumes to speak for God. They may ask God's blessing for what they do, but they do not—and cannot—invoke the authority of Christ or Moses or any other deity or prophet to compel Americans to do what the individual may demand. When an Islamic cleric speaks, he speaks for both law and religion and his congregation hears in that context. Muslim imams—clerics, sheikhs, and others who presume to religious authority such as bin Laden, Hizballah's leader Nasrallah, and their ilk—must be understood as not mere political speakers. Their words are intended to carry the weight of the Muslim religion and their listeners are expected to believe and obey. Every statement by a Muslim leader carries a weight of authority that is the sum of mosque and state. They invoke God not to bless what they do but to demand subordination to their will.

From the Palestinian West Bank and Gaza Strip, from the holiest mosques in Mecca and Medina in Saudi Arabia, in Iran, on television, radio, and from hundreds of other podiums, the factories of hate produce a steady stream of anti-American invective that prescribes terrorism against Americans, Israelis, Britons, and every other people who are not subjects of radical Islam. The hate factories have been operating in plain sight, in many languages, spreading the ideology of Islamofascism and producing the terrorists who fight against freedom. They are an immediate danger, and they have been so for years.

Sheikh Ahmed Yassin, the so-called "spiritual leader" of the Hamas terrorist organization, was killed in an Israeli strike in 2004. Almost six years earlier, he spoke to the Al-Quds newspaper about Saudi support and the need for "martyrdom operations"—i.e., suicide bombings. Here are some excerpts from that interview:[1]

QUESTION: Was the fact that the King of Saudi Arabia received you during your tour of the Arab states a message to the United States?

YASSIN: It was an expression of appreciation on the part of Saudi Arabia for [our] activities for the sake of Palestine and to

tell the world—especially the U.S. and Israel—**that Saudi Arabia supports the path of jihad**. Saudi Arabia has demonstrated strength and courage because it declared its position loud and clear, telling the U.S. that it supports the path of struggle to restore the plundered land. In other words, the welcome I received was a clear message to the U.S. and a provocation against its policy. . . .

All Arab peoples and leaders support the Palestinian people, and the entire trip was a provocation against the American policy in the Middle East.

QUESTION: Has your position toward Iran changed as the result of your visit to Tehran?

YASSIN: Yes, my position changed. I did not know that the Iranians were so interested in the Palestinian cause. I found in them a deep willingness to liberate Palestine—a will to endure for the Palestinian cause all the hardships created by the U.S. policy.

QUESTION: But the position of the Muslim Brotherhood in Palestine [meaning the Hamas movement] used to be anti-Iranian. Has it changed?

YASSIN: From the moment that the Islamic revolution broke out in Iran, we supported it. But there were those who wanted to present the situation as if the Iranians were the jihad warriors while we evaded [our duty].

QUESTION: Have you been promised financial assistance from governments or individuals?

YASSIN: We were promised financial assistance from both governments and individuals to support the Palestinian people. They promised to support humanitarian and educational institutions of the Palestinian people, as well as Palestinian prisoners

and the families of martyrs.... The promise still stands and we
are waiting for it to be realized.

QUESTION: Do you expect Israel to attempt to assassinate you?

YASSIN: I will be very happy if that happens. I wish they had done
it already—if they have the talent for it. The day in which I
will die as a shahid [martyr] will be the happiest day of my life.

*This same theme appears again and again in the Palestinian
mosques—and in print and on television—in the Friday sermons,
the most important because they are given on the eve of the Muslim
Sabbath. We hear it time and again from clerics such as Sheikh
Ibrahim Mahdi.*[2]

*The Friday sermons are broadcast each week live on Palestinian
Authority television. One week after the suicide bombings in Tel Aviv
and only days after Yasser Arafat's declaration on the cease-fire,
Sheikh Ibrahim Mahdi gave this sermon and called for "martyrdom
operations" and the destruction of Israel, the U.S., and Britain:*

... the era preceding the end [of days] has began—the era of the
military rule, the era of revolutionary rule. Allah willing, we are at
the end of this era and Allah willing, the Caliphate will return, in
accordance with the prophecy, and I pray that we will be among
its soldiers....

Allah is almighty. Had He wanted—He would have beaten
them. But He tests you in suffering. We must prepare the ground
for the army of Allah that is coming according to the [divine] pre-
determination. We must prepare a foothold for them. Allah willing, this unjust state will be erased—Israel will be erased; this
unjust state, the United States, will be erased; this unjust state,
Britain, will be erased—they who caused this people's Nakbah
[the 1948 "catastrophe"]....

Blessings to whoever waged Jihad for the sake of Allah; blessings to whoever raided for the sake of Allah; **blessings to whoever put a belt of explosives on his body or on his sons' and plunged into the midst of the Jews**, crying "Allahu Akbar, praise to Allah, There is no God but Allah and Muhammad is His messenger."

Just as the building collapsed over the Jews in their sinful dancing floor [referring to the collapse of a wedding hall in Jerusalem]—I pray to Allah that this oppressive Knesset will collapse over the heads of the Jews.

Allah, forgive us our sins, show us a black day for the Jews, like the day of 'Aad and Thamud. Allah, turn them into pillage for us....[3]

The following is an editorial from Al-Manar, a Palestinian weekly, published in August 2001, titled: "Bush and His Stupid Dreams" (courtesy of MEMRI):[4]

In his hostility towards our Palestinian people and its leadership, George Bush has gone further than any other leader of the country which claims to be neutral or host to the peace process....

This is, by no means, a praise to the American presidents who preceded him. Each and every one of them had his role in serving the Zionist goals in the region and in the world in its entirety. However, some of them ... kept in mind that the huge number of Arabs and Muslims may lose control, and the [Arab] rage may cross the red lines—leading to the flattening out of some of Washington's embassies to ground level, or to the shelling and burning of some of its military vessels in the ocean, along the Arab shores....

The stupidity of [the Palestinian] people's enemies, the likes of Bush and Sharon, who cruelly attack headquarters, commanders, and members of the Palestinian security apparatuses, double the momentum of the linkage between all the parts of the united body which forms the Palestinian people, and first and foremost, the symbol and leader of its struggle, President Yasser Arafat.

Two months before September 11, the Qatari international television station, al Jazeera, broadcast a special episode of its Opposite Direction program titled: "Bin Laden: The Arab Despair and American Fear." The host, Faisal Al-Qassem, debated bin Laden with critic, London resident, and Sudanese author Al-Hatem 'Adlan and a bin Laden supporter, Abd Al-Bari 'Atwan, editor-in-chief of the London daily paper Al-Quds Al-Arabi. Al-Bari spoke in favor of bin Laden having interviewed him personally. (The translators at MEMRI prepared a special report on this in December 2001. They discussed the "bin Laden phenomenon." As you read this debate, consider that the point is not that polls—real or imaginary—show support for bin Laden or terrorism against America. The point is that these debates go on almost every day across the Islamic world, yet most Americans remain in the dark about how the power of the media is being harnessed by our adversaries.

Here are some excerpts from the debate:[5]

'Adlan opened the discussion by stating that he perceived the "bin Laden phenomenon" as "part of a broader phenomenon of international terrorism...the main goal of which is to seize power by violent means."

'Atwan disagreed: "If you want to talk about terrorism against a legitimate government, fine. The U.S. dropped two atom bombs on Nagasaki and Hiroshima, and the victims were innocent.... This is the legitimate power you are defending. Didn't it kill hun-

dreds of thousands of innocent people? Can we call this government legitimate? It is a terrorist regime that has killed innocent
people since 1945 to this very moment.... In Vietnam, did they
kill innocent people or not?"

Al-Qassem told his guests that many viewers had sent faxes to
the studio saying: "In light of the terrible Arab surrender and self-
abasement to America and Israel, many of the Arabs unite around
this man, who pacifies their rage and restores some of their trampled honor, their lost political, economic, and cultural honor...
[Because of the] leadership vacuum, many listen to a man like bin
Laden." Later in the show, a viewer, Dr. Sa'ad Al-Faqih, a known
Saudi Islamist living in London, went on the air, saying, amongst
other things, that "the Muslims, primarily the rulers, provide outstanding examples of treachery, weakness, and submission to the
Americans...."

"The nation thirsts deeply for someone who will confront
America...not with words and slogans. [The nation thirsts] for
someone who can prove in practice that he is a worthy opponent.... Bin Laden [became] the right man for this important role
in the confrontation with America, the enemy of the Muslims,
which conspires with the Muslim rulers to hurt [the Muslim
nation] and plunder its resources. Bin Laden is an ordinary man,
like anyone else...he weighs little and his influence is limited....
**But America's arrogance and conceit prevent it from
understanding the truth about the Islamic world and
about how Muslims think.** There is a tremendous cultural and
psychological barrier between America and the Muslims...."

'Adlan said he supported Hizbullah and Hamas, but not terrorism against America: "Although America supports Israel, America cannot be seen only from this angle.... We are opposed to the

American position on Israel and fight it in this area. But we cannot, for example, fight trade with America; we can't try to topple the American government on behalf of the American people. This [would be] is a real mistake . . . let the American people topple whomever—Bush, Clinton—that's their business."

"You present bin Laden as if he wanted to topple the [government in] America and take it over," interjected host Al-Qassem. "All the man wants is to expel America from the region."

"You called bin Laden 'America's oppressor,' and said that he made the Americans 'flee like rats,'" replied 'Adlan. "I think this is absolutely untrue."

"How can you say it's not true?" Al-Qassem protested. "Don't you watch television? The U.S. Navy cancelled a joint maneuver with Jordan, fled Bahrain, all those things. . . . Can you deny that this Jihad warrior who is now in Afghanistan [bin Laden] is striking fear into America, which shudders at the sound of his name?"

'Atwan, who had throughout the program claimed that bin Laden has no intention of destroying America but only of bringing about its expulsion from the Middle East, asked that bin Laden's influence on the American public not be underestimated: "The U.S. spent $2 billion on increasing security at its embassies . . . . The American citizens are terrified. Every day there's an alert: 'Don't go out at night, go in groups, don't vacation in these places. . . . ' Sixteen embassies closed in a single day because of a threat, or half-threat, by bin Laden. It's no exaggeration. It's reality."

Host Al-Qassem kept up the pressure on 'Adlan: "Can you deny that Osama bin Laden or his associates managed to destroy the American military bases. . . . They hit a few dozen of them, making the Americans conceal their bases in remote places in the middle of the desert. [Look at the case of] the destroyer USS *Cole* in Yemen. As everyone knows, a green fly cannot get to these destroyers—not even mighty Russia can get to them—but he got to it [USS *Cole*] and destroyed it.... Today, when two people talk on the telephone—and as everyone knows, the American satellites monitor even the crawling of ants—and one says to the other, bin Laden is going to carry out a bombing soon, all of America goes on high alert. What more do you want? The guy strikes fear into the entire world."

"I think," said 'Adlan, "that the chances of Osama bin Laden's toppling the American regime don't even approach one in a million. These are extremely marginal matters. It's a very serious issue, because it will make America treat bin Laden and groups like him as if they had declared war [on America], and handle them not through legal investigation inquiry, but with the American armed forces...."

'Atwan did not back down: "There is a phenomenon of Arabs and Muslims willing to die a martyr's death. They are willing to die, willing to blow themselves up, and this is what America fears. America has taken over the world with so-called globalization. It has taken over the world economically by means of the big banks; it has taken it over in the security sense by means of the treacherous regimes...and it has taken it over in the media sense by means of the mighty arms of the media, such as the Internet and satellite channels. The only thing capable of ruining this globalization is armed actions against the embassies...as the American military is unbeatable [in direct confrontation]...."

Concluding the program, host Al-Qassem said: "Al-Hatem 'Adlan, there was an opinion poll in a Kuwaiti paper which showed that 69 percent of Kuwaitis, Egyptians, Syrians,

Lebanese, and Palestinians think bin Laden is an Arab hero and an Islamic Jihad warrior...65 percent claimed that attacking American targets was justified, because it [is implementation of the principle of] 'an eye for an eye,' and because the American slogan is 'Might is Right'...76 percent would be sorry if bin Laden were caught. You demand democracy and such things—here's democracy for you. This is [the opinion of] the people. Besides, I have a poll on the [Al-Jazeera] Internet site. Out of 3,942 people who responded, 82.7 percent saw bin Laden as a Jihad fighter, 8.8 percent as a terrorist, and 8.4 percent didn't know. This is an actual result about which there can be no argument.... There is an Arab consensus from the Gulf to the [Atlantic] ocean. A real 82 percent—not like percentages in elections in Arab countries."

Consider this: in the Islamic world there are few—if any—media outlets that are not government-controlled. Because governments— such as the terrorist sponsors in Syria, Iran, and other nations— control the information going to their populations, what they present is the "mainstream" media. There is no opposition press. Terrorist sympathizers in the press beget more terrorism. What we do not observe—and absorb—in the ideological war, we cannot answer. And we do not.

Perhaps the most violent and hate-inspiring sermons come from Saudi preachers. MEMRI published this summary and translation of a number of Saudi preachers' words in 2002. These sermons are pure Islamofascist ideology. They are more than just the ravings of street corner preachers. These are the official sermons, written and read by the government-backed Wahabbi clergy, that are a key part of the Saudi state. Because they are official, they are tantamount to Saudi government statements.[6]

The following sermons target the "infidels"—Christians and Jews.

Delivered at the Al-Salaam mosque in 'Al-Unayzah by Sheikh Abd Al-Muhsin Al-Qadhi:

"Today we will talk about one of the distorted religions, about a faith that deviates from the path of righteousness...about Christianity, this false faith, and about the people whom Allah described in his book as deviating from the path of righteousness. We will examine their faith, and we will review their history, full of hate, abomination, and wars against Islam and the Muslims.

"In this distorted and deformed religion, to which many of the inhabitants of the earth belong, we can see how the Christians deviate greatly from the path of righteousness by talking about the concept of the Trinity. As far as they are concerned, God is the Father, the Son, and the Holy Ghost: three who are one....

"Regardless of all these deviations from the path of righteousness, it is possible to see many Muslims...who know about Christianity only what the Christians claim about love, tolerance, devoting life to serving the needy, and other distorted slogans.... After all this, we still find people who promote the idea of bringing our religion and theirs closer, as if the differences were miniscule and could be eliminated by arranging all those [inter-religious] conferences...."

Delivered at the Qabaa mosque in Al-Madina by Sheikh Abd Al-'Aziz Qari:

"Two groups—the Jews and the Christians—are the main elements constituting the 'Camp of Kufur' and will continue to be its two foundations until Allah allows their downfall and annihilation at the end of days...."

"When the Prophet Muhammad was sent out, the 'Camp of Kufur' declared war on his message. At the center of this war were these groups, particularly the Jews. These two groups will continue to serve as the grindstones of the conflict and the war between belief and Kufur until eternity comes.... The conflict will end when Jesus the son of Mary, peace be upon him, arrives to break the cross and wipes it off the face of the earth, and kills the blind [false] Messiah, the leader of the Jews and the tyrant whom they await. Until that day, the conflict between us, the Muslims, and the Jews and Christians will continue, and it will ebb and flow, one day ours, another day theirs....

"The Jews are the objects of Allah's [promised] wrath, while the Christians deviate from the path of righteousness.... The Koran described the Jews as a nation cursed by Allah, a nation at which he was angry—some of whom he turned into apes and pigs...."

In a sermon delivered at a Mecca mosque, Sheikh Adnan Ahmad Siyami condemns inter-faith harmony:

"[Islam] believes that only Islam and the 'Camp of Kufur' exist, and that there is no way to reach Paradise and to be delivered from Hell except by walking in the path of our Prophet Muhammad and joining Islam. Any other way leads to Hell.... In light of this, my believing brethren, how can it be claimed that Judaism, Christianity, and Islam are all paths leading to Allah?!

"Several years ago, a sinful call arose, which unfortunately garnered support from some clerics and preachers of this religion, Islam... [a call] for the unification of the monotheistic religions. They flaunted an empty and false slogan of 'religious harmony,' Christian-Islamic friendship, and uniting the three religions into a global religion....

"The call for the unification of the religions is a call for the abolition of religious differences among people: No more Muslim and infidel. All will come under the unity of human harmony.... This accursed call has ramifications that most certainly will shake Islam in the hearts of its people, leading them to the lowest of the levels of Hell. This call will lead...to presenting the infidels' schools of thought as correct, and to silence regarding them; to permitting conversion to Judaism and Christianity with no shame whatsoever; to the abolition of the vast difference between the Muslims and others—a difference underpinning the conflict between truth and falsehood; to the transformation of the religion of Islam into a religion like the other, false religions, into a religion that has no advantage over the other religions...to refraining from calling [people] to join Islam, because if the Muslim wants to do so, he must tell the truth about the infidels.... This will also facilitate the conversion to Christianity in Muslim lands.

"The Pope's recent visit to Syria, to the Al-Umawi mosque is, without a doubt, another manifestation of that call. **The call by [the Pope]—may Allah punish him as he deserves—to the people of the [different] religions in Syria to live in peaceful coexistence is nothing more than an audacious call for the unification of religions**, in accordance with the principle of human religious harmony.... This Pope, the head of the Catholic Church, and those behind him calling for the unification of the religions, are the descendants of the Spanish inquisitors who tortured the Muslims most abominably.... They are the descendants of those who led the Crusades to the Islamic East, in which thousands of Muslims were killed and their wives taken captive in uncountable numbers. They are the perpetrators of the massacres in Bosnia-Herzegovina...in Kosovo, in Indonesia, and

in Chechnya.... Can we expect compassion from these murderous wolves? What made the Pope go on his visit was his dissatis-
faction with the robbing of the Muslims' lands; he wanted also to
rob their religion, so that they lose both this world and the Here-
after....

"[This is]... a call to dismantle the pact among Muslims in all
the corners of the Islamic world and to replace it with an accursed
alternative harmony—the 'Harmony of the Jews and Christians.'
This is, in truth, a call to Muslims to stop accusing Jews, Christians, and other non-Muslims of being infidels....

"**There can be neither an agreement nor a meeting
point between the people of Islam and the Jewish and
Christian People of the Book.**... How can we allow the
Catholic Pope's talk of a need to find meeting points and agreement
between Islam and Christianity, so that there will be peaceful coexistence between the two religions and harmony between the two
communities? Is it conceivable that there should be agreement and
a meeting point with those who fabricate terrible falsehoods about
Allah... claiming that Jesus, peace be upon him, is his son?!..."

Delivered at a Mecca mosque, Sheikh Mustafa Bin Sa'id Aytim
also condemned inter-faith harmony:

"It is no surprise that the Jews and Christians deny the Koran.
What is amazing is that some ignoramuses and traitors from
among the Muslims say: 'The Jews and Christians are our brothers....' It is quite amazing that anyone claiming he believes in the
Koran says that the Jews and Christians love us and feel no
loathing and hatred for us!... The People of the Book's hatred of
Muslims is certain and absolute. This is a solid belief, which Allah
has proven in the Koran, and there is also historical evidence of

it.... And lo, today we see that they lie about security and peace—a security council here, a peace emissary there; a security plan here, a prayer for peace there. By Allah, who told you that wild animals can become human? Can wild animals give birth to anything other than wild animals?"

Delievered at the Manar Al-Islam mosque in Mecca by Sheikh 'Ali Muhammad Al-Baroum:

"The idea of intertwining religions and the claim that the Jews and the Christians believe in religions of truth... are sinful claims and deceitful ideas unacceptable to the religion [of Islam]... It is forbidden to bring together Islam and the infidels, monotheism and polytheism... Allah's path of righteousness and Satan's path of Kufur."

Delievered at Al-Rahmah mosque in Mecca by Sheikh Marzouq Salem Al-Ghamdi:

"Some may say: 'How can the inventor of electricity be placed in Hell—he illuminated the world for us.' Others may say, 'How can we be hostile to the Jews and Christians when they invented and manufactured even the items we use in our mosques?' Yet others may say, 'The messenger of Allah left his shield with a Jew and went to visit his sick Jewish neighbor. Why do you preach to us to do differently?' The truth is that this is an inversion of the facts, and deception. The Jew whom the Prophet considered a citizen had accepted the agreement [that the Prophet Muhammad had concluded with the Jews of Al-Madina]... and when his people violated that pact, and supported the polytheists instead of the Muslims, their punishment was death, captivity, and the expropriation of their assets.

"If the infidels live among the Muslims, in accordance with the conditions set out by the Prophet, there is nothing wrong with it provided they pay Jizya to the Islamic treasury. Other conditions are... that they do not renovate a church or a monastery, do not rebuild ones that were destroyed, that they feed for three days any Muslim who passes by their homes... that they rise when a Muslim wishes to sit, that they do not imitate Muslims in dress and speech, nor ride horses, nor own swords, nor arm themselves with any kind of weapon; that they do not sell wine, do not show the cross, do not ring church bells, do not raise their voices during prayer, that they shave their hair in front so as to make them easily identifiable, do not incite anyone against the Muslims, and do not strike a Muslim.... If they violate these conditions, they have no protection."

These sermons describe the clash of civilizations—the struggle for leadership of mankind.

Delivered by Imam of the Al-Haraam mosque in Mecca Sheikh Abd Al-Rahman Al-Sudayyis:

"The most noble civilization ever known to mankind is our Islamic civilization. Today, Western civilization is nothing more than the product of its encounter with our Islamic civilization in Andalusia [medieval Spain] and other places. The reason for [Western civilization's] bankruptcy is its reliance on the materialistic approach, and its detachment from religion and values. [This approach] has been one reason for the misery of the human race, for the proliferation of suicide, mental problems... and for moral perversion....

"Western civilization's credibility as the one capable of leading the world to happiness and man to stability—is shaken.... Only one nation is capable of resuscitating global civilization, and that is the nation [of Islam]. . . . No decent man in the world will deny that there has never been a culture more merciful towards [all] creatures, with more supreme values, and which rules with greater justice than [Islam]. . . . While the false cultures sink in the swamp of materialism and suffer moral crises . . . our Islamic nation is the one worthy of grasping the reins of leadership and riding on the back of the horse of pioneering and world sovereignty.

"When this happens, our nation will not use cultural progress as a tool for exploiting the peoples, exhausting their resources, and dishonoring them. It will not use [scientific] inventions and discoveries to spread secularism and support terror. . . . It will not use military equipment and war technologies as an excuse to threaten the security of countries and peoples, or for barbaric and wild operations, and it will not recruit the media to mislead public opinion. . . . The Islamic message, whose aim is to save the human race and to bring about happiness for man who is today lost in the dark tunnels of injustice and misery. . . takes this burden upon itself. . . ."

Delievered by Saudi Arabia's Grand Mufti Sheikh Abd Al-'Azia Aal Al-Sheikh at the Nimra mosque in 'Arafa:

"Those who attack Islam and its people—what have they given to the human race?! What have they to be proud of?! They gave a false, contemptible culture; they gave various kinds of damage to [human] freedoms and rights on the pretext of preserving these values; they gave discrimination among people by color, gender, language, and race; they gave technology to create weapons of mass destruction for the destruction of the human race; they gave forms of deceit and falsehood. . . ."

Homosexuality is addressed by Sheikh Sa'd Bin Abdallah Al-
'Ajameh Al-Ghamdi at the Sa'id Al-Jandoul mosque in Al-Taif:

"This act is not alien and uncommon to the brothers of mon-
keys and pigs [i.e., Jews] and the debased among the infidels. . . .

"It shocked me to read and hear about the audacity of the
'Betrayer-General' of all nations [a reference to the UN Secretary-
General], who by affiliation and loyalty is a combination of a Jew
and a Christian and leads the people to Hell. He called to stop the
incursion of this disease called AIDS—although two months earlier he had contradicted this call when, in stupidity and brazen-
ness, he led the nations calling for permissiveness that causes this
disease. He called for permitting adultery and spreading acts of
abomination and homosexuality, which is a sexual perversion, and
even invited this kind of people to a conference in order to call for
permitting them marriage of the third kind. . . . "

*The Jews are often referred to as "apes and pigs"—based upon a ref-
erence in the Koran—and are often the subject of sermons in Saudi
Arabian mosques. MEMRI notes that when preachers are discussing Jews they "base their sermons on Koranic history, as well as
on pseudo-historic events which affirm the Koranic view."*

Delivered by Sheikh Mustafa Bin Said Aytim at a mosque in Mecca:

"Oh Muslims, see the state of the nation today, after it deviated
from the path set out by the clerics. [The nation] has made the offspring of apes and pigs its stars; the hangers-on of the apes and
pigs have become the centers of influence and power. . . . The Jews,
Christians, and the hypocrites gnaw away at the body of the nation
and then carry out raids on it with the knights of the destructive
media and with the deadly weapon of globalization. . . . "

Delievered by Sheikh Abd Al-Muhsin Al-Qassem at the Al-
Nabawi mosque in Al-Madina:

"They spilled the blood of [the prophet] Yahya, sawed Zacharia
in two, planned to kill Jesus, and tried several times to kill
Muhammad....The Jews are ingrates, whoever treats them well
they harm, and whoever treats them with honor they rebel against.
Allah saved them from drowning with Moses [at the Red Sea];
they did not thank Allah, but arrogantly and haughtily asked
Moses to make another god for them instead of Allah, so they
could worship it as they wished....

"They annihilated people and nations with usury....They consume the Muslims' resources by destroying their economy, and
introduce prohibited things into trade. They harm Muslims so as
to bankrupt them. They seek to cause them poverty....In their
own eyes, they are Allah's chosen people, and they see others as
slaves created to meet their needs.

"Their tongues never cease lying, [disseminating] abomination and obscenity. About Allah they said: 'His hands are tied....
He is poor and we are wealthy.' They brought great disasters upon
Jesus and his mother, and of the Prophet Muhammad they said:
'He is a trickster and a liar.' Curses were laid upon them, one
after another, and punishments too....The Jews preached permissiveness and corruption, as they hid behind false slogans like
freedom and equality, humanism and brotherhood. They kill
Muslim youth, entice the [Muslim] woman with shameful deeds,
and act to lure others through her....They defile the minds of
adolescents by arousing their urges...they are envious of the
Muslim woman who conceals herself and protects her honor; for
this reason, they preach to her to expose herself and throw off her
values....Their goal is to destroy the Muslim family, to shatter

religious and social ties and foundations.... They are cowards in battle...they flee from death and fear fighting.... They love life...."

Delivered by the Imam of the Al-Harram mosque in Mecca, Sheikh Abd Al-Rahman Al-Sudais:

"Brothers in faith, what do our Koran and our Sunna say? What does our belief say? What does our history prove...? They show clearly that the conflict between us and the Jews is one of belief, identity, and existence....

"Read history and you will understand that the Jews of yesterday are the evil forefathers of the even more evil Jews of today: infidels, falsifiers of words, calf worshippers, prophet murderers, deniers of prophecies...the scum of the human race, accursed by Allah, who turned them into apes and pigs.... These are the Jews—an ongoing continuum of deceit, obstinacy, licentiousness, evil, and corruption....

"Oh nation of Islam, today our nation is at the height of conflict with the enemies of yesterday, today, and tomorrow—the offspring of [the three Jewish tribes of Al-Madina] Banu Qurayza, Banu Nadhir, and Banu Qaynuqa, upon whom Allah's curse rests until Judgment Day. Do the sons of our people realize the truth about the nation of wrath and deceit...? The insult to and contempt of Arabs, Muslims, and their holy places reaches its height at the hands of the rats of the world, the violators of agreements, in whose minds abide treachery, destruction, and deceit and in whose veins flow occupation and tyranny.... They are indeed worthy of the curse of Allah, of the angels, and of all people...."

Delivered at the Al-Nour mosque in Al-Khobar by Sheikh Nasser Muhammad Al-Ahmad:

"In the Jews, an astonishing quantity of moral abomination and corrupt behavior has accumulated. These cannot exist in any other nation. What is amazing is that this corruption in all things concerning morality, and this impudent behavior, are not limited to a specific generation of Jews, or to a specific group of Jews, but are manifest in the distorted Jew everywhere. Every Jew, except for the prophets and the believers among the [ancient] Children of Israel, is a human model of the same moral traits, from which the contemptible Jew who lived in the time of Pharoah or the liberated Jew who lives today on the land of Palestine, is not spared.

"Moral corruption is a general trait of the Jews, all the Jews. [These are] stable hereditary genes [found] in the Jew in every time and in every place. If you want to know the Jew through and through, imagine a group of perverse moral traits....

"The Jews are liars...in their religious life, in their ritual, in the way they see Allah. The Jews lie to their enemies and friends alike.... What is strange is that they have turned the lie into a religion, a faith, and a ritual through which they draw closer to their god.... If we say that they speak the truth this time [regarding the peace process], it would mean that we are denying the Koranic text—a very serious matter....

"Most of the world's wars, particularly the great modern wars, were planned and started by the Jews so as to disseminate corruption in the land, and to achieve their goals on the ruins of the human race.... I will conclude the matter of these moral traits with something else connected to the Jews: The Jews are an accursed nation. This is part of our belief. We believe that the Jews are accursed...."

Delivered by Sheikh Mushabbab Fahd Al-Qahtani at the 'Ubad Al-Rahman mosque in Al-Zahran:

"The desire to corrupt the people is present also in the Jews of our time. See the great interest-charging banks, the cinemas, the alcohol factories, the drugs, the tobacco companies, the fashion houses, the sex networks, the secret organizations—the Jews are behind them."

Delivered by Sheikh Abd Al-'Aziz Qari at the Qaaba mosque in Al-Madina:

"In ancient times, the Jews, the enemies of Allah, killed the prophets unjustly.... Afterwards they became the enemies of all humanity and they [termed] non-Jews 'gentiles,' and used all means to destroy them by starting wars among these gentiles, destroying their beliefs, and corrupting their moral values....

"See for example, how they show the woman on television and on the front pages of the newspapers. They show her without modesty or shame, made up and exposing her curves, with the aim of destroying and corrupting the nation's general moral values.... They exploited the woman in the most abominable way. And this is a known Jewish conspiracy...."

These sermons discuss the theme: "It is Impossible to Make Peace with the Jews."

Delivered by Sheikh Nasser Muhammad Al-Ahmad at Al-Nour mosque in Al-Khobar:

"There is no doubt that the [Muslim] nation is today reaping the fruit of agony because of its renunciation of its honor on the day it begged [peace] at the negotiating tables, chasing after a false peace that could never be. Because, in all honesty, these are people with whom no agreement or pact can be made...."

"[Muslims] should have never been led under any pressure of any kind towards the so-called peace process, which is in effect a process of surrender. The Muslims should have acted...as their forefathers did when they faced the Crusader's occupation of Palestine for over ninety years, and nevertheless did not surrender....

"The events proved that no one has the authority to make Palestinian decisions except for the Palestinian masses, and that **these crimes [against the Palestinians and the Muslims] will be stopped only by Jihad.** The sites holy to Muslims will be regained only by Jihad for the sake of Allah....When true Islamic Jihad is declared, the balance of power will shift. What frightens the West more than anything else is the word Jihad, because they understand what it means....

"Humiliation and misery will be the lot of the ones who anger Allah, who cursed them and turned them into apes and pigs.... There is no solution to this problem, and to any problem to which the infidel enemy is party, except by waving the banner of Jihad."

A sermon delivered by Sheikh 'Adel Bin Ahmad Bana'ma at the Muhammad Al-Fatih mosque in Jiddah:

"For the thousandth time, the [Islamic] nation is losing its memory and sits with its enemy to discuss peace, agreements, and treaties....The Jews themselves do not forget their hatreds. **Today, they disseminate everywhere the lie of the Holocaust and claim that Hitler killed six million Jews in gas chambers.** Although this is pure falsehood, they have made it part of their history of trials and tribulations, disseminated it with their mighty propaganda machine, and extorted the countries of the world with it. They obtained huge reparations from Germany with it, and still accuse everyone who denies it of anti-Semitism, and incite the world against him. [The French Holocaust denier] Garaudy's story happened not long ago!"

For Saudi preachers, jihad is the only way of solving the problems of Islamic nations.

"Who would have believed it?!" cried Sheikh Sultan Al-'Uweid in a sermon at the Prince Tareq mosque in Al-Damam. "A handful of brothers of apes and pigs torments a billion [Muslims].... There is no other way, oh Muslims, but restoring the missing precept— Jihad for the sake of Allah.... There is no other way but educating to Jihad...."

Sheikh Muhammad Saleh Al-Munajjid delivered the following at a mosque in Al-Damam:

"The issue is historic, religious, and ideological. It is impossible ever to make peace with the Jews; we must not [enter into] a pact with them, we must not [sign] a treaty with them— despite those [among us] who maintain otherwise, who are Jews just like the Jews. There is no hiding from the evil of the Jews; there is no concealment from their deception. The Jews are defiled creatures and satanic scum. The Jews are the helpers of Satan. The Jews are the cause of the misery of the human race, together with the infidels and the other polytheists. Satan leads them to Hell and to a miserable fate. The Jews are our enemies and hatred of them is in our hearts. Jihad against them is our worship...."

The following sermons discuss the indoctrination of children:

Sheikh Muhammad Saleh Al-Munajjid spoke about educating children to Jihad:

"Muslims must . . . educate their children to Jihad. This is the greatest benefit of the situation: educating the children to Jihad and to hatred of the Jews, the Christians, and the infidels; educating the children to Jihad and to revival of the embers of Jihad in their souls. This is what is needed now. . . ."

"Manliness" must be developed in children's souls, argued Sheikh Majed 'Abd Al-Rahman Al-Firian at the Suleiman Bin Muqiran mosque in Al-Riyadh:

"One of the ways of developing manliness in the personality of the children is to tell them of the heroic deeds of our forefathers; of the Islamic battles; and of the Muslim victories, so that courage will develop in their souls—as courage is one of the most important traits of manliness.

"Zubeir Bin Al-'Awwam had two children. . . . One of them would play with the scars of his father's wounds after the battles. . . . His [other] son, Abdallah participated with his father in the battle of Al-Yarmouk, and when the polytheists were defeated he . . . completed the killing of anyone he found wounded—which attests to the courage of his heart, even in his youth."

Sheikh Wajdi Hamza Al-Ghazawi dismissed that education to jihad is education to terrorism in a sermon at the Al-Manshawi mosque in Mecca:

"The [kind of] terror [in Arabic, 'striking of fear'] that Islamic religious law permits is terrifying the cowards, the hypocrites, the secularists, and the rebels by imposing punishments according to the religious law of Allah. . . .

"The meaning of the term 'terror' used by the media . . . is Jihad for the sake of Allah. Jihad is the peak of Islam. Moreover, some of the clerics . . . see it as the sixth pillar of Islam. Jihad—whether Jihad of defense of Muslims and of Islamic lands such as in Chechnya, the Philippines, and Afghanistan, or Jihad aimed at spreading the religion—is the pinnacle of terror, as far as the enemies of Allah are concerned. The Mujaheed who goes out to attain a martyr's death or victory and returns with booty is a terrorist as far as the enemies of Allah are concerned. . . . Accordingly, the believer must not use this word. . . . Jihad, oh believers, is an integral part of our religion. The word 'terror' is used to damage this mighty and blessed foundation. . . . "

In Saudi sermons, preachers place special emphasis on the Islamic nature of the Palestinian cause. The national Arab movement is often ridiculed and condemned by Saudi preachers, who insist that the only way to liberate Palestine is through jihad.

Sheikh Muhammad Saleh Al-Munajjid delivered a sermon at an Al-Damam mosque where he said:

"The [Palestinian] cause is exploited by hypocrites, the secular, polytheists, and pan-Arabs. . . . They must be silenced, disregarded. We must unite around those who talk of the Islamization of the cause. . . . If we say that the cause is an Arab cause, there are among us Christian Arabs, and infidels . . . and Socialists. What do all these have to do with Al-Aqsa Mosque?!"

Sheikh 'Abd Muhsin Al-Qadhi's sermon at the Al-Salaam mosque in Al-'Unayza discussed this issue, saying that,

"We must recognize that one of the reasons for our defeat by the Jews is that the [Islamic] nation was not allowed to confront them. . . . Our nation must know that our defeats by the Jews were the defeats of regimes that did not wave the banner of Islam. They waved any banner except for the banner of Islam. . . .

"If those who have gone astray return to the truth, the Jews will return to the humiliation and misery to which they were sentenced [by Allah]. . . . Then, nothing will help the Jew[s]. . . . They will not see victory as long as they persist with misleading concepts, heretical curricula, and a shameful 'peace of the brave.' All this is the seed of Satan and the seedling of the infidels, and it is this which prevents the victory of Allah and throws a lifeline to the Jews."

Sheikh Majed 'Abd Al-Rahman Al-Firian proclaimed in a sermon at the Suleiman Bin Muqiran mosque in Al-Riyadh:

"The modern countries of Kufur [that is, Western countries] have realized that the [Palestinian] Authority that speaks today on behalf of the Palestinian cause has not waved the banner of Islam, and its goal is to establish a secular state. Therefore, they protect it and prohibit attacking it, as [this authority] is the one that will give them concessions when they pressure it. In contrast, the alternative to this authority arouses fear in their hearts. This is a deep-rooted solution to the conflict: Intifada and Jihad for the sake of Allah, not for the sake of pan-Arabism, and not for the sake of protecting the homeland and the soil. Today, the Islamic nation already knows that the Holy Land will not be liberated by dallying at vacation sites or sitting around the negotiating table with infidels. The solution is to do what the Prophet did to the Jews when they violated the agreements. . . . **The solution regarding the Jews is as the Prophet Muhammad said: 'I have brought slaughter upon you'. . . . Yes, the solution for these is not peace and harmony. . . . Jihad, not peace, is the solution.**

"The one who retreated and surrendered to Judaism and Christianity is not Islam, but secularism. The one who threw down its weapon and sought to surrender was not Islam but secularism. Islam was not defeated by Judaism and Christianity in the ideological battle because it was prevented from entering it."

One major point of conflict between Islam and the West discussed by Saudi Imams is the status of women, which is perceived as a matter of life and death for Muslim society. The Saudi preachers see the West's preoccupation with the status of women in Islamic countries as an attempt to undermine and topple Islamic society.

Sheikh Muhammad Al-Nimr delivered a sermon at the Al-Huweish mosque in Al-Taif where he said:

"The enemies of Islam . . . know that the woman is a double-edged sword, and that she can be transformed into the most dangerous weapon of destruction [of Islamic nations]. Thus, the woman has suffered from most of the conspiracies to shatter the Islamic nation—because the woman has a group of traits allowing her to either build or destroy the nation. . . .

"The enemies of Islam have decided to distance the Muslims from their religion. Therefore, they have made the woman the most important weapon in this destruction. Ostensibly, they are showing her mercy and defending her rights. Many among the Muslim women have been misled by this, because of their ignorance about their religion, which sees the woman as the man's partner and as possessing rights and obligations appropriate to her nature and character. . . .

"Permitting women to leave the home, so that they rub up against men in the marketplaces and talk with people other than their chaperones—with some even exposing parts of their bodies prohibited from exposure—are forbidden acts, a disgrace, and lead to destruction. The first crime perpetrated by the Israelites was letting their women loose when they were adorned, so that they would stir up Fitna [inner strife]. For this, Allah punished them with the plague."

Sheikh Mansour Al-Ghamdi's sermon at the Abu Bakr Al-Siddiq mosque in Al-Taif contained this language:

"The Muslim who is aware of what is happening can connect the prodigious attack on men's and women's modesty and morals.... with the Jewish plan to destroy their humanity and make them look like animals—that is, exposed and naked."

To illustrate the danger of female permissiveness, the preachers often cite "historical" examples of societies that collapsed in its wake. Sheikh Mansour Al-Ghamdi said:

"The enemies realized that the woman is a mighty and important fortress of the Muslim nation, and that for centuries this fortress protected the strength of Islamic society....

"The enemies learned the lesson of what happened to the Greek and Roman societies, which collapsed because of the women's corruption. When these cultures began, the woman was protected and modest, and engaged in housework.... Then [the Greeks and Romans] succeeded in their conquest, establishing mighty empires. When the woman began to beautify herself, and to go out to clubs and public places ... she corrupted the moral values of the men, weakened their combat skills—and their civilization collapsed. Yes, these two mighty cultures collapsed, and [the enemies] maintain that the Muslim nation must collapse in such a way that will make it incapable of recovery. This is the strategic goal towards which the enemies of the Muslim nation strive, as is written in the Protocols of the Elders of Zion.... The enemies of the Muslim woman are the Jews, the Christians, the hypocrites, the secular, and the opportunists trailing behind them."

Sheikh Muhammad Abdallah Al-Habdan's sermon at the Al-'Izz Bin Abd Al-Salaam mosque in Al-Riyadh is another example:

"I warn of the danger [inherent] in the woman if she deviates from the divine path. The man can be steadfast in many battles, but surprisingly the same giant man often founders in the face of the woman and her enticements.... The main reason for the downfall of Paris and the French army's swift surrender to the German armies, as historians have acknowledged, was overindulgence in urges and immersion in pleasure....

"Why do the West and the secular Westernizers focus on the [Muslim] woman? The answer is that they grasped the status of the woman and her role in the building of the nation, and her influence on society, and therefore realized that if they corrupt the woman and manage to entice her into deviating from the path of righteousness, it will facilitate their infiltration of the Muslim strongholds.... The satanic Jews say in their Protocols: 'We must get the woman. The day she stretches out her hand to us is the day of our triumph....'"

Another way preachers illustrate the imminent danger to Islamic women is by showing the "downfall" of the Western woman. Sheikh Fahd Bin Abd Al-Rahman Al-'Abyan spoke at an Al-Riyadh mosque, saying:

"Some people have been influenced by the putrid ideas spread by the infidel West about the [Islamic principle of] man's custodianship over the woman. On the face of it, these ideas appear to protect the woman's rights. But in truth, their goal is to push the people into sinful liberty that has caused the downfall of [entire] societies. [In the West] this false liberty has engendered a society with crime as its hobby, adultery as its entertainment, and murder as its means of sublimating rage; a society in which the number of illegitimate children approaches and sometimes even surpasses the number of children from permitted unions . . . a society in which the woman does as she pleases even if she is married . . . a society in which underage girls know and do what married women know and do, and even more. . . . These putrid ideas—no more than conceptual trash disseminated by the West—have begun to appear in the whorish journals and on the [Arab] satellite channels. . . .

"[In the West] the woman leaves the home whenever she feels like it, goes where she wants, and wears what she wants, without her husband's permission. Furthermore, in some homes the situation has reached the point where the woman gives the orders, and that is that. . . . It is no wonder, then, that the [Western] women have become masculine. But what is amazing is that some men have become feminine. You can see some husbands with nothing in common with men except external appearance, while the woman calls the shots and controls the children's fate without asking her husband's opinion, even without consulting him or informing him of her intentions. . . ."

In a sermon at the Al-Basateen mosque in Al-Riyadh, Sheikh Saleh Fawzan Al-Fawzan spoke about the plight of Western women:

"In [Western] societies, the woman has become cheap merchandise, displayed naked or half-naked before the eyes of men. . . .

Women are servants in homes, clerks in offices, nurses in hospitals, hostesses on airplanes and in hotels, teachers of men in schools, film and television actresses. If they do not succeed in presenting the woman in these ways, they present her voice on the radio, as an announcer and a singer. . . . As is known, the number of women in society surpasses the number of men. Nevertheless, they have limited marriage to a single wife, abandoning the rest of the women to corrupt and be corrupted. . . .

"They travel unsupervised and live as strangers among strangers, with danger threatening from all sides. Thus, the enemies of Allah and of humanity have stripped the miserable woman of all the elements of a happy life and of all her social rights, so that she serves as a tool of corruption and destruction. You will be surprised to hear that in spite of these crimes, they claim that they are protecting the woman's freedom."

According to the preachers, the status of the Muslim woman is far better not only than that of Western women, but also than that of women in any other culture.

"In India," Sheikh Mansour Al-Ghamdi asserted in a sermon at the Abu Bakr Al-Siddiq mosque in Al-Taif, "the woman has no right to independence from her father, husband, or son. . . . She must die the day her husband dies, and be burned alive, together with him, on the same pyre. In China, a man has the right to sell his wife as a slave. If a Chinese woman is widowed, her husband's family has the right to her, as property. A Chinaman has the right to bury his wife alive. . . .

"Western culture waves around empty slogans about women's liberation, women's equality with men, and no controlling of women. In the wake of these slogans, the woman has left her home . . . lives a life of misery, and is burnt in the fire of this false liberty. . . . Acts of abomination have proliferated in an unprecedented manner . . . and they are no longer restricted to the brothels, but are also committed in hotels, cafes, dance clubs, and even on the roads. It is no longer considered strange or perverse for a father to lie with his daughters, or a brother with his sister. . . . "

At the same time, many sermons instruct women how to behave so as not to slide down the slippery slope of the "moral degradation" pervasive in the West. The sermon of Sheikh Hamad Ibrahim Al-Hariqi at Al-Basateen mosque in Al-Riyadh is one example of many:

"One of the mistakes made by women with regard to their husbands is to avoid [joining] the husband when he calls her to bed claiming that she is fatigued, or simply because she wants to anger him, or because she is ignorant and does not know that by doing so she denies her husband the greatest of his rights and places herself under serious threat. . . . As it was said: 'If a man calls his wife to his bed and she refuses to come, the angels curse her until she wakes up. . . .'

"Another mistake is deficient service to her husband. If she does not fulfill his needs, such as cooking, laundering, keeping the house clean, and the like, it is because she is lazy and for no other reason. There is no doubt that this is a grave thing. [These tasks] are the woman's right and obligation towards her husband . . . . The wise Muslim woman must take care of and serve her husband, in a way that will gladden him and cast happiness between them.

"Another mistake is to allow entrance to anyone whom the husband does not permit to enter the home. The husband has the right to bring only the people he likes into his home, and the woman must obey him. She has no right to bring in anyone he hates, even if it is her relatives.... When the husband takes other wives, some women behave with exaggerated jealousy, ignorance, and stupidity."

In Saudi Arabia, the ruling family claims ancestry of Mohammad ibn Abdul Wahhab, the eighteenth-century fundamentalist preacher who founded the Wahhabi sect that rose to rule what was then called "the Nejed" and is now Saudi Arabia. How did they rule?

British Lieutenant General Sir John Bagot Glubb learned first-hand as a young RAF officer stationed in the Iraqi desert in the mid-1920s. His job was to defend the Shia tribes of southern Iraq against Wahabbi raiders coming out of the Nejed called, "Al Ikhwan"—the brotherhood—which is the forebear of a current group based in Egypt. Glubb researched his Wahabbi opponents' history and said that, before dissolving in Napoleonic times and then reviving in the mid-nineteenth century, they ruled with a heavy hand and a military he described as "primitive":

Their policy of wholesale massacre, however, induced such terror that conquered populations hesitated to revolt, even if left without a garrison of [Wahabbis]. The Wahabbis murdered in cold blood every male human being, even small children, but women were rarely, if ever, molested.[7]

That history, as former Israeli UN ambassador Dore Gold points out, is not only ancient but part of the modern. In his book Hatred's Kingdom, Gold describes a 1978 booklet published with the official seal of the Kingdom of Saudi Arabia on its cover. The booklet, "The

Methods of the Ideological Invasion of the Islamic World," was:

...written by two Saudi lecturers at the Islamic University of Medina for students of Islamic law and *da'wa* (missionary work). In their introduction, the authors argued that the West raised the flag of secularism: "In the economic field that means the flag of capitalism, in the political field that means the principles of democracy, and in the social field it waves the principles of freedom." The West, they claimed, was invading Islamic society in order to undercut the values of Islam. To counter this ideological invasion, the authors argued, strong Islamic states must be established, and the *ummah*, the Islamic nation, must be strengthened. They described secularism in education and the mass media as "aggression against Islamic legitimacy." To the authors, the West was nothing less than the enemy of Islam; there could be no coexistence.[8]

And, Gold concludes, this is the same message we hear again and again from Osama bin Laden.

Though Saudi Arabia is a primary source of Islamofascist ideology, it is not the only one. The Saudi ruling class, and its religious speakers, are Sunni Muslim. Across the Persian Gulf is Iran, another principal source. And—with its pursuit of nuclear weapons—the biggest danger.

THREE

The Hate Networks

The Islamist radicals preach not only in mosques and schools. They feed on each others' hate and recruit on the Internet. The Islamist websites are a constant source of information for law enforcement and—occasionally—for military intelligence. What they reveal is the fanaticism of the radicals.

The following excerpts from some Islamist websites should be read in the context of the Democrats' hell-bent desire to force the withdrawal of American troops from Iraq and the legislation proposed by Democratic senator Jim Webb of Virginia in early 2007 to provide a legislative prohibition to attacking Iran. Does the new enemy want to win more than we do? Apparently, they do. Their war against us knows no limits, and purposefully rejects the limits on warfare established by the Geneva Conventions. Consider the al Qaeda charter and training manual that have been found and published by the White House and the U.S. Air Force:

AL QAEDA CHARTER

There Will Be Continuing Enmity Until Everyone Believes In Allah. We Will Not Meet [The Enemy] Halfway And There Will Be No Room For Dialogue With Them.[1]

AL QAEDA TRAINING MANUAL

Guidelines for Beating and Killing Hostages: Religious scholars have permitted beating. . . . In this tradition, we find permission to interrogate the hostage for the purpose of obtaining information. It is permitted to strike the nonbeliever who has no covenant until he reveals the news, information, and secrets of his people. The religious scholars have also permitted the killing of a hostage if he insists on withholding information from Moslems.

Islam does not coincide or make a truce with unbelief, but rather confronts it. The confrontation that Islam calls for with these godless and apostate regimes, does not know Socratic debates, Platonic ideals nor Aristotelian diplomacy. But it knows the dialogue of bullets, the ideals of assassination, bombing, and destruction, and the diplomacy of the cannon and machine-gun.[2]

These are the words of Sheikh Abdel Rahman, planner of the first World Trade Center bombing, whose statements were smuggled out of a U.S. prison:

Oh, you Muslims everywhere, sever the ties of their nation, tear them apart, ruin their economy, instigate against their corporations, destroy their embassies, attack their interests, sink their ships, and shoot down their airplanes. Kill them in land, at sea, and in the air; kill them wherever you find them.[3]

At its core, the war waged by the Islamofascists against our way of life is an ideological one. We are failing to engage the enemy on this front. We do not take on the ideology that is radical Islam. And even when we do, we do not take it far enough.

Case in point: the State Department–sponsored Arabic language television channel, Al-hurrah, which broadcasts to the Middle East. Instead of pouring unvarnished news into the eyes and ears of Middle Easterners, Al-hurrah began tilting toward the worst of the radical Islamist terrorists. In early 2007, it gave two hours of programming to Hizballah terrorist chief Nasrallah to explain his ideology to whomever could be reached. American taxpayers' money could be much better spent.

By contrast, the Islamist television networks and Internet sites frequently give the terrorists free rein to sell hate. In June 2002, nine months after September 11, a number of websites (and perhaps Arab language newspapers) published this article by al Qaeda's second in command, Ayman al-Zawahiri: "Why We Fight America: Al-Qa'ida Spokesman Explains September 11 and Declares Intentions to Kill 4 Million Americans with Weapons of Mass Destruction."

Al Qaeda spokesman Suleiman Abu Gheith, originally from Kuwait, recently posted a multi-part article titled "In the Shadow of the Lances" on the website of the Center for Islamic Research and Studies, www.alneda.com. Following numerous hacking attempts after the international media reported that the site was linked to al Qaeda, its address was changed to http://66.34.191.223.

The following are excerpts from Abu Gheith's article:

PART I: WHY WE FIGHT THE U.S.

".... Perhaps the [Islamic] nation is waiting for one Al-Qa'ida man to come out and clear up the many questions that accompany any communiqué, message, or picture [concerning September 11], to know the truth, the motives, and the goals behind the conflict with the Hubal [one of the pre-Islamic Ka'ba idols—referring to the U.S.] of our generation...."

"Why is the world surprised?! Why were millions of people astounded by what happened to America on September 11? Did the world think that anything else would happen? That something less than this would happen?!"

"**What happened to America is something natural, an expected event for a country that uses terror, arrogant policy, and suppression against the nations and the peoples**, and imposes a single method, thought, and way of life, as if the people of the entire world are clerks in its government offices and employed by its commercial companies and institutions."

"Anyone who was surprised, and did not expect [the events of September 11] did not [understand] the nature of man, and the effects of oppression and tyranny on man's emotions and feelings. They thought that oppression begets surrender, that repression begets silence, that tyranny only leaves humiliation. Perhaps they also thought that this [oppressive] atmosphere is sufficient to kill man's virility, shatter his will, and uproot his honor. These people erred twice: once when they ignored [the consequences of] treating man with contempt, and again when they were unaware of man's ability to triumph."

"This goes for every man—let alone when the man in question is of those who believe in Allah, in Islam as a religion, and in Muhammad as Prophet and Messenger, and anyone who knows that his religion is unwilling to allow him to be inferior and refuses to allow him to be humiliated."[4]

The following two paragraphs need to be read and re-read separately. Think of how Suleiman Abu Gheith's rhetoric echoes in the history of the twentieth century.

PART II: THE ENTIRE EARTH MUST BE SUBJECTED TO ISLAM

"How can [he] possibly [accept humiliation and inferiority] when he knows that his nation was created to stand at the center of leadership, at the center of hegemony and rule, at the center of ability and sacrifice? How can [he] possibly [accept humiliation and inferiority] when he knows that the [divine] rule is that the entire earth must be subject to the religion of Allah—not to the East, not to the West—to no ideology and to no path except for the path of Allah? . . ."

"As long as this Muslim knows and believes in these facts, he will not—even for a single moment—stop striving to achieve it, even if it costs him his soul . . . his time, his property, and his son, as it is said, 'Say [to the believers]: If your fathers and your sons and your brethren and your wives and your kinsfolk and the worth you have acquired and the trade, the dullness of which you apprehend, and the dwellings that you fancy are dearer to you than Allah and

His Messenger, and striving in His cause, then wait until Allah issues His judgment. Allah guides not the disobedient people...."[5]

We are too quick to disregard this sort of violent hate speech. The West was traumatized by the same sort of claim to mastery when Hitler spoke of the Aryan "master race." We ignore precisely this same claim from the Islamofascists because the memory of what it cost to defeat Hitler is too painful to contemplate. Before we dismiss Suleiman Abu Gheith's claim that Islam has a right to rule the earth, we must remember how costly it has been for us to fight him and those like him. And how much more costly will it be if we ignore him even now? Read the rest and decide for yourself:

PART III: THE BLOW AGAINST THE U.S. WILL COME FROM WHERE LEAST EXPECTED

"....The [premises] on which we base ourselves as an organization, and on which we base our operations and our method of action, are practical and realistic.... They are also scientific and [in accordance with] Islamic religious law, and they give us confidence and certainty.... In writing them and in [publicly] revealing them, I do not intend to be apologetic for what was done; I lay [these arguments] before you so as to emphasize that **we are continuing with our blows against the Americans and the Jews**, and with attacking them, both people and installations [so as to stress] that what awaits the Americans will not, Allah willing, be less than what has already happened to them. **America must prepare itself; it must go on maximum alert.... because, Allah willing, the blow will come from where they least expect it....**"

"America is the head of heresy in our modern world, and it leads an infidel democratic regime that is based upon separation of religion and state and on ruling the people by the people via legislating laws that contradict the way of Allah and permit what Allah has prohibited. This compels the other countries to act in accordance with the same laws in the same ways ... and punishes any country [that rebels against these laws] by besieging it, and then by boycotting it. By so doing, [America] seeks to impose on the world a religion that is not Allah's. ..."

"America, with the collaboration of the Jews, is the leader of corruption and the breakdown [of values], whether moral, ideological, political, or economic corruption. It disseminates abomination and licentiousness among the people via the cheap media and the vile curricula."

"America is the reason for all oppression, injustice, licentiousness, or suppression that is the Muslims' lot. It stands behind all the disasters that were caused and are still being caused to the Muslims; it is immersed in the blood of Muslims and cannot hide this."

"For 50 years in Palestine, the Jews—with the blessing and support of the Americans—carried out abominations of murder, suppression, abuse, and exile. ... The Jews exiled nearly 5 million Palestinians and killed nearly 260,000. They wounded nearly 180,000, and crippled nearly 160,000."

"Due to the American bombings and siege of Iraq, more than 1,200,000 Muslims were killed in the past decade. Due to the siege, over a million children are killed [annually]—that is 83,333 children on average per month, 2,777 children on average per day. 5,000 Iraqis were killed in one day in the Al-'Amiriya shelter alone...."

"In its war against the Taliban and Al-Qa'ida in Afghanistan, America has killed 12,000 Afghan civilians and 350 Arab Jihad fighters, among them women and children. It annihilated entire families from among the Arab Jihad fighters while they were in their cars, when the American Air Force bombed [them] with helicopters and anti-tank missiles, until nothing remained of some of them except scattered body parts."

"In Somalia, America killed 13,000 Somalis and [its soldiers] carried out acts of abomination on [Somali] boys and women...."

Part IV: The Islamic Justification for al Qaeda's Jihad against the U.S.

"The religious arguments on which we base ourselves in our Jihad against the Americans—the explanations that inspire us with confidence in the triumph of our religion, our belief, and our faith—are many, and this is not the place to enumerate them, as they are included in the books of the sages...."

"In this article I will present one explanation that suffices [to wage] Jihad against the Americans, the Jews, and anyone who has gone in their path...."

"Allah said, 'He who attacked you, attack him as he attacked you,' and also, 'The reward of evil is a similar evil,' and also, 'When you are punished, punish as you have been punished....'"

Part V: Islamic Law Allows
Reciprocation against the U.S.

"If by religious law it is permitted to punish a Muslim [for the crime he committed]—it is all the more permitted to punish a *Harbi* infidel [i.e., he who belongs to *Dar Al-Harb* 'the domain of disbelief'] in the same way he treated the Muslim."

"According to the numbers I noted in the previous section of the lives lost from among the Muslims because of the Americans, directly or indirectly, we still are at the beginning of the way. The Americans have still not tasted from our hands what we have tasted from theirs. The [number of those] killed in the World Trade Center and the Pentagon were no more than fair exchange for the ones killed in the Al-'Amiriya shelter in Iraq, and are but a tiny part of the exchange for those killed in Palestine, Somalia, Sudan, the Philippines, Bosnia, Kashmir, Chechnya, and Afghanistan."[6]

Here again, pay closest attention to Zawahiri's words. He speaks of "rights" to kill millions of women and children and to use chemical and biological weapons. When Americans withdraw from Iraq, will the war be over? No. To paraphrase Churchill, it will not even be the beginning of the end of the war between Islamofascism and the West. But it may be the end of the beginning.

Part VI: We Have the Right
to Kill Four Million Americans

"We have not reached parity with them. We have the right to kill four million Americans—two million of them children—and to exile twice as many and wound and

cripple hundreds of thousands. **Furthermore, it is our right to fight them with chemical and biological weapons, so as to afflict them with the fatal maladies that have afflicted the Muslims because of the [Americans'] chemical and biological weapons.**"

"America knows only the language of force. This is the only way to stop it and make it take its hands off the Muslims and their affairs. America does not know the language of dialogue!! Or the language of peaceful coexistence!! America is kept at bay by blood alone. . . ."[7]

The Islamofascist propaganda machine regards the fight against America as one and the same as the fight to destroy Israel. They made that entirely clear a year before September 11. The following is a list of excerpts from a Friday sermon in the Zayed bin Sultan Aal Nahyan mosque in Gaza. The sermon was delivered by Dr. Ahmad Abu Halabiya and was broadcast live on Palestinian Authority television. Dr. Ahmad Abu Halabiya is a member of the PA-appointed "Fatwa Council" and former acting rector of the Islamic University in Gaza:

. . . . None of the Jews refrain from committing any possible evil. . . . The Jews are Jews. . . . They do not have any moderates or any advocates of peace. They are all liars. They all want to distort truth, but we are in possesion of the truth.

O brother believers, the criminals, the terrorists—are the Jews, who have butchered our children, orphaned them, widowed our women and desecrated our holy places and sacred sites. They are the terrorists. They are the ones who must be butchered and killed, as Allah the Almighty said: "Fight them: Allah will torture them at your hands, and will humiliate them and will help you to overcome them, and will relieve the minds of the believers...."

O brothers in belief, this is the case of the Jews and their habitual conduct, and what happened yesterday, and has been going on for two weeks, and before that for many years, and which will be repeated in future years unless we stand up like men and unless we have the known Muslim position, [the position] of those who wage Jihad in the path of Allah, those who defend their rights and who sacrifice all that is dear to them.

O brothers in belief, the beautiful bride has a costly price and dowry.... Our bride is paradise, O brothers in belief.... The cost and the dowry of this bride, the dowry of this paradise, is that we fight in the path of Allah, and kill and be killed....

.... We say to the Jews, and we say to Clinton, and we say to all those who supported the Jews and still cooperate with the Jews, we say to them, that this will not shake us, we are the Palestinian people, who are positioned in the land of the Isra' and Mi'raj. It will not shake a single hair of ours. Our determination will not sway. We will raise the banner of Jihad....

.... America and Europe and the world were shocked by the kidnapping of three tramps, the kidnapping of three wretched soldiers, and the killing of two in Ramallah. But their feelings were not moved, and they did not shudder when they saw the children Muhammad ad-Durrah and others—women, and men, and youths—being martyred by cannons and missiles, and all the barbaric instruments that the Jews possess.

They were moved, for the sake of five persons, and the world went into turmoil and it will not stop for Clinton or for the old hag Albright, they will not be relieved, and they will not cease to be concerned, and they will not rest until the Jews return to their families. But as for the Palestinians, as for this pure blood, it can go to Hell in the eyes of the Americans and Europe and the Jews....

....The Jews are the allies of the Christians, and the Christians are the allies of the Jews, despite the enmity that exists between them. The enmity between the Jews and the Christians is deep, but all of them are in agreement against the monotheists—against those who say, 'There is no God but Allah and Muhammad is his messenger,' that is—they are against you, O Muslims."

....None of the factions is allowed to stand on the sidelines at this stage, or not to think well of avenging our pure martyrs and wounded....Our people must unite in one trench, and receive armaments from the Palestinian leadership, to confront the Jews. By Allah, the Jews, O brothers in belief, do not know, nor have they ever known throughout history, anything but force and Jihad in the path of Allah. The Jews are like a [gas] pedal—as long as you step on it with your foot, it doesn't move, but if you lift your foot from it, it hurts you and punishes you. This is the case of the Jews.

Have no mercy on the Jews, no matter where they are, in any country. Fight them, wherever you are. Wherever you meet them, kill them. **Wherever you are, kill those Jews and those Americans who are like them**[2]—and those who stand by them—they are all in one trench, against the Arabs and the Muslims—because they established Israel here, in the beating heart of the Arab world, in Palestine. They created it to be the outpost of their civilization—and the vanguard of their army, and to be the sword of the West and the crusaders, hanging over the necks of the monotheists, the Muslims in these lands. They wanted the Jews to be their spearhead....

....Let us put our trust in Allah, close ranks, and unite our words, and the slogan of us all should be, "Jihad! Jihad! For the sake of Palestine, and for the sake of Jerusalem and Al-Aqsa!"

...Allah, deal with the Jews, your enemies and the enemies of Islam. Deal with the crusaders, and America, and Europe behind them, O Lord of the worlds....[8]

FOUR

The Hate Networks Aim at Iraq

Part of the ideological war is centered in Iraq, aimed at stirring up and continuing the Sunni insurgency and Shiite militias to fight coalition forces and prevent the nascent democracy in Iraq from taking root. Here is a sampling of what the al Qaeda terrorists and others are doing, continuously, to foment violence in Iraq.

According to a MEMRI report, on February 3, 2007, Islamist websites posted a twenty-three-minute audio recording by Emir Al-Muaminin ("Commander of the Believers") Abu Omar Al-Baghdadi. Al Qaeda appointed him "head of the Islamic State of Iraq." This is a transcript of the recording from the MEMRI website. It is titled, "Victory from Allah, Victory Is Near," and was issued by the Islamic State's media company Al-Furqan on February 2, 2007:

We [hereby] inform the Sunnis of a [new] plan called the Plan of Honor, which is more comprehensive and more perfect [than the existing plan] and includes not only Baghdad but all parts of the Islamic State [of Iraq].... **[This plan] will end with Bush**

**announcing the failure of his [security] plan and signing
an agreement of defeat.** . . . The goals of the plan are: to defend
our people and our honor; to rout out the invaders and eradicate
the remaining pockets and bases of heresy; to butcher the
wounded Crusader tyrant and take advantage of the collapse of
morale among [the Crusader] soldiers and commanders; to unite
the ranks of the mujahideen and to strengthen the foundations of
the Islamic State [of Iraq].

Oh Muslim youths, remember the cut up bodies of the children, the voices of their bereaved [parents] and the anguished
cries of the elderly. Let the volcano of your wrath burst forth. Burn
the ground beneath the feet of the Jews and their helpers, eradicate their army, destroy their equipment, down their planes,
ambush them in their homes, in the wadis and on the roads. Hide
in the darkness of night and turn their morning into hell . . . We are
not afraid of your coalitions. . . . We have drunk blood [in the past],
and we find no [blood] sweeter than that of the Byzantines [i.e.,
Christians]. . . . Roast their flesh with car bombs, cut off their supply lines with [explosive] charges and tear out their hearts with
sniper fire. Know that offense is the best [form of] defense, and
be careful not to lay down your weapons before the war is over. . . .
We are not fighting out of nationalism, but with the aim of making Allah's word supreme. . . .

Your brother,

Abu Omar Al-Qurashi Al-Husseini Al-Baghdadi

Muharram 14, 1428 [February 2, 2007][1]

*Faced with the surge of American forces into Baghdad, the terrorist
hate networks praised the preparation of attacks:*

ISLAMIST VIDEO SHOWS PREPARATION,
EXECUTION OF SUICIDE ATTACK IN MOSUL

On March 8, 2007, Islamist websites posted a fourteen-minute video titled "The Martyrdom Operation in Mosul," produced by the media company of the Ansar Al-Sunna organization. The video shows the planning and execution of a suicide attack in the city of Mosul in northern Iraq.

The film opens with the caption "Martyrdom Operation Carried Out by Brother Abu Al-Bara Al-Shami against a Peshmerga Facility in Mosul," and then shows the mujahid giving his last message before setting out on the operation. Following this, several jihad fighters are shown preparing explosive charges.

The next scene is introduced by the caption "The Brothers' Last Meal with Abu Al-Bara," and shows him dining and then taking leave of his companions. This scene also shows the inside of the vehicle used in the attack.

The third caption gives details about Abu Al-Bara, saying: "Abu Al-Bara was the youngest son in his family. He told us that his mother loved him very much because he obeyed her and used to help her with the housework. A few days before he set out on the operation, his brothers the jihad fighters called his family in Syria, and he spoke with his mother and told her: 'I bought a car and I am getting betrothed today. My brothers are with me and they are preparing to accompany me to the marriage ceremony.' His mother replied, with tears in her voice: 'Oh my son, do as you wish, and as Allah is my witness, I wish you and your brothers every success. Go on [your way], and may

Allah bless you.' Next, he spoke with his brothers and sisters and told them to obey Allah . . . and after finishing this call, he set out on the operation."

The attack itself is shown from two different angles: from in front of the vehicle and from behind. The vehicle is seen moving towards the building and exploding next to it. The video reports that the mujahideen attacked when the building was full in order to maximize the number of fatalities, and that thirty-five "apostates" of the Peshmerga forces were killed.

The video can be viewed at: http://switch3.castup.net/cunet/gm.asp?ClipMediaID=678139&ak=null.[2]

The hate networks spew not only al Qaeda propaganda, but also propaganda from the Pakistani Inter-Service Intelligence organization that established—and still protects and maintains—the Taliban. Once again, from MEMRI:

ISI SPOKESMAN: "ONLY BY ROLLING SKULLS AND SPILLING BLOOD WILL WE ACHIEVE VICTORY"

On March 11, 2007, Islamist websites posted an 8.5-minute video by the official ISI spokesman, titled "The Failure of the Al-Maliki-Bush Plan." The spokesman, whose face is masked, says that Bush has not achieved victory in Iraq, since his forces suffered heavy losses and are now in retreat, while the strength of the jihad fighters is steadily growing and their victory is near. The spokesman also called upon the people of Baghdad not to lay down their weapons, but to fight to the death. The following are excerpts from the speech:

"With the help of the apostates, Bush waged many battles in Iraq, under different names, but he achieved no victory.... In spite of this, he remains arrogant and stubborn and continues his series of crimes....

"Our Islamic nation, you have seen the [achievements] of the jihad fighters and the defeat of the Crusaders and apostates, from the downing of their planes and the killing of their pilots, to the arrest and execution of dozens of interior ministry employees, ... and the killing of many dozens of Crusaders. The losses suffered by the enemies of Allah are constantly increasing and exceed [all] forecasts....

"Our beloved nation, there is no better evidence for the failure of the so-called 'Security Plan' than the attack carried out by your sons, the ISI soldiers, on Badush prison in Mosul province—which is run by the apostates under Crusader supervision—and the release of over 150 of our brothers the prisoners.

"We remind everyone that [only] by rolling skulls, spilling blood, and continuing [the jihad] will we achieve victory and [find] salvation—not [with the help] of neutral international forces or the so-called 'Arab League' or the 'Baghdad Security Conference,' in which all the forces of heresy, from near and far, formed an alliance....

"Oh brothers, [people of] Baghdad, beware not to lay down you weapons and leave [Baghdad] to your enemies.... Do not lay down [your weapons] until your souls have departed your bodies.... With your endurance and your jihad you defend your honor and your lives, and [bring about] the revival of the Caliphate....

"Our beloved Islamic nation, know that the infidels have begun to retreat and to flee, while Islam is on the rise."

The video can be viewed at: http://switch3.castup.net/cunet/gm. asp?ClipMediaID=677997&ak=null.[3]

As the next excerpt from MEMRI demonstrates, the pressure on Iraq is relentless:

IRAQI MILITANT GROUP "THE ARROWS OF GOD" THREATENS TO KILL TWO GERMAN HOSTAGES IF GERMANY DOES NOT WITHDRAW ITS TROOPS FROM AFGHANISTAN WITHIN TEN DAYS

In a video posted March 10, 2007, on Islamist websites, an Iraqi militant group calling itself "The Arrows of God" presented footage of two German hostages and issued an ultimatum to the German government. The tape opens with hostage Hannelore Marianne Krause, her son by her side, imploring the German government to comply with the ultimatum or else the capturers "will kill my son in front of my eyes and then kill me," and appealing also to the general public and NGOs to pressure the government to comply. She stresses that her son recently married and his wife could be pregnant.

The film then shows three masked mujahideen, one of whom reads out an ultimatum to the German government: if it does not announce the withdrawal of its troops from Afghanistan within ten days "it will not see even one corpse" of the hostages.

The video can be viewed at: http://switch3.castup.net/cunet/ gm.asp?ClipMediaID=678078&ak=null.[4]

Mujahideen Issue a Video Ultimatum to Germany and Austria to Withdraw Their Troops from Afghanistan

In a six-minute video accompanied by German subtitles, produced by the Global Islamic Media Front (GIMF) and presented via the "Caliphate Voice Channel," the mujahideen issue an ultimatum to Germany and Austria to withdraw their troops from Afghanistan or suffer the consequences. Throughout the film, a masked mujahid is seen addressing the German and Austrian governments, telling them that Germany's and Austria's presence in Afghanistan does not serve the two countries' interests but rather benefits "Bush's war against Muslims."

The speaker criticizes Germany's claims that its presence in Afghanistan prevents attacks from being carried out inside Germany, saying that Germany has not been targeted by the mujahideen in the past, but will be targeted if it persists in its military involvement in Afghanistan. The speaker says that such involvement only jeopardizes the flourishing economies of both Germany and Austria. The speaker concludes with an ultimatum to both countries that if their troops are not withdrawn from Afghanistan soon, their economic interests worldwide will be attacked by the mujahideen.

The video can be viewed at: http://switch3.castup.net/cunet/gm.asp?ClipMediaID=680105&ak=null.[5]

The statements below were made in September 2004, accompanying a video showing the beheading of American hostage Eugene Armstrong:

The mujahideen will give America a taste of the degradation you have inflicted on the Iraqi people....[6]

Oh Allah, America came with its horses and knights to challenge Allah and his Messenger.... O Allah, rend the kingdom of Bush as you rent the kingdom of Caesar.... O Allah, curse the Arab tyrants and the foreign tyrants; O Allah, strike the apostate rulers; O Allah, kill them one after the other, sparing none.[7]

This is a telling excerpt from a documentary about Abu Musab al Zarqawi. The speaker is al Zarqawi's former cell mate, Nasser Nassef:

As for fighting the Americans we base ourselves on the Koran. When the nation reads in the Koran: "retaliation is prescribed for you," it is considered justice; "fasting is prescribed for you," we all fast. And when it says: "fighting is prescribed for you," we must all fight. Is it clear that we must fight the Americans? By Allah it is clear as day. The Americans are a nation that corrupts the land. They say this, not me. They say: "We are corrupting the land." People, the satanic corruption of the land takes the form of institutions that rule the land. These institutions—a whole day would not suffice to describe them—the UN, the Security Council, the IMF, the CIA. Their sole raison d'être is to corrupt the land, and Allah does not like the corrupters. Instead of discussing where al Zarqawi is right or wrong—and by Allah, he's right—I'd like to talk about George Bush, who corrupts the land. America bears within the roots of its own destruction because of its war against Allah and because of its corrupt policies. I am absolutely certain the day the dollar collapses, I mean the collapse of the bills, the stocks

and the bonds, like has happened to the airlines and the oil and
communications companies, the American will discover he has a
pile of papers.... This Great Satan occupies the world
through.... Here is a slogan I'd like the whole nation to repeat
tonight: "**America is a weak as a spider web and the White
House is the weakest house.**"[8]

*Below is part of a speech given by al Zarqawi that was downloaded
by MEMRI from al Qaeda's Jihad Media Battalion website:*

This battle came at this time in order to cover up the scandal of
Allah's enemy, Bush, in his dealing with what was left behind by
one of Allah's soldiers—the devastating Hurrican Katrina, which
revealed to the entire world the great helplessness in dealing with
the destruction caused by this hurricane, because of the tremendous attrition of the American army's resources in Iraq and
Afghanistan. This hurricane has once again brought to the mind
the manifestations of racial discrimination among the American
people. And has exposed the fragility of the foundations upon
which it's structured. The acts of assault and killings have spread,
as well as robbery and looting and what is still to come will be
even more terrible, Allah willing. This battle has come in order to
unveil the ugly face of the government of the descendants of Ibn
Al-Alqami and to remove the shield behind which they hide.[9]

*The excerpts below have been compiled by MEMRI and are from a
new al Qaeda weekly Internet news broadcast, Sout Al-Khilafa:*

We now move on to the occupied land, to the land of the
Caliphate, the glorious land of Iraq. The American wolves, and

behind them the Rafidite Shiite dogs, have desecrated our
(women's) honor in Tel'afar and other Sunni cities, while the Muslims and the scholars of the Sultans keep silent. The valiant hero,
the Emir of al Qaeda in Iraq, Abu Mus'ab al Zarqawi, rose to
defend the honor of the pure Muslim women in the robbed land
of Iraq. In two consecutive communiqués, he declared the beginning of the Sunni vengeance raid.

The entire Islamic world overflowed with joy when Hurricane Katrina struck in America, which seemed to reel from the
strength of the hurricane and went asking for aid from all the
countries of the world. Broken and completely humiliated,
George Bush, a fool who is being obeyed, announced his obvious incapability to deal with the wrath of Allah that visited the
city of homosexuals.

While Louisiana is trying to recover from the aftermath of
Hurricane Katrina, another hurricane fiercely struck the state of
North Carolina, on the Atlantic coast, but so far there have been
no casualties or significant damage, as was expected. We hope
that Allah will humiliate America with this hurricane to make it a
lesson for whoever wants to listen.[10]

In the 2006 mini-war between Israel and Hizballah forces in southern Lebanon, Israel suffered a strategic defeat. It hesitated, advanc-
ing and pulling back again and again, without destroying the
Hizballah forces entirely and preventing them from re-arming.

The Hizballah war against the United States, like the other terrorists with whom they make common cause, makes clear that its
principal enemy is America. Sheikh Nasrallah, the commander of
Hizballah, makes that clear at every opportunity. Nasrallah said in
a statement aired on Beirut Al-Manar Television in September 2002:

"Let the entire world hear me. Our hostility to the Great Satan is absolute.... Regardless of how the world has changed after 11 September, Death to America will remain our reverberating and powerful slogan: Death to America."[11]

Almost a year before that war broke out, the *"martyrdom seekers"* were on the warpath against Israel and the United States.

"MARTYRDOM SEEKERS" MOVEMENT IN IRAN
AL-ARABIYA TV (DUBAI) JULY 2, 2005

WOMAN: My name is Vresaly.... We are first and foremost Muslims, and it's our duty to defend our brothers and sisters thoughout the world. We don't need permission from anyone. This has to do with our religious duty and responsibilities. This is our choice, and we have no fear. We adhere to the legacy of our late leader Imam Khomeini.

CHANTING: There is no God but Allah, and Muhammad is Allah's messenger.

VOICEOVER: These young women have forsaken the temptations of life, and have chosen the hard way. Indeed they have chosen martyrdom as a way of liberating the Islamic lands. This is what they say. 40,000 time bombs in Iran—this is the number of volunteers so far and the registration is still open. There is no distinction between men and women, Sunnis or Shiites. "We all sacrifice for the sake of Islam," they chant. This is the movement of the martyrdom seekers, whose goals and organizational structure are still unclear. They refuse to give further details, but did not conceal their determination to sacrifice their lives. The reason: What America has done in the holy places of Najaf and Karbala....

ALI SAMADI (one of the movements leaders): As everyone can see, the Zionists attribute no significance to the Arab and Islamic governments. They continue their aggressive policies to fulfill their goals. The world considers the Israeli military to be the world's fifth most powerful force, and its security apparatus is to be the second most powerful in the world. Since they only understand the language of force, our new weapon of martyrdom operations is bound to change the balance of power.... We are not afraid of the American fleets or the British weapons in Iraq. We vow to become time bombs in the event of any aggression in our land.

VOICEOVER: Thus they await death with happiness and joy. In their view martyrdom for the sake of Allah is the sweetest thing.

Must-see Saudi TV II

From the day civil strife began in Islam the Jews were behind it. There is no evil in the world that the Jews are not behind. No evil in the world. Search in the east or in the West, near or far in the depths of history and in the future and you will find that the finger of the Jews of the Jewish Masonry is behind everything. They attempted to corrupt Christianity and they attempted to corrupt Islam.

IQRA TV EXAMINES PUBLIC ATTITUDES TOWARDS JEWS

Iqra TV Saudi Arabia September 26, 2004

Q: Would you as a human being, be willing to shake hands with a Jew, and why?

MAN ON THE STREET 1: Of course I wouldn't be willing to shake
hands with a Jew, for religious reasons and because of what is
happening now in Palestine, and for many reasons that don't
allow me to shake a Jew's hand.

MAN ON THE STREET 2: No, because the Jews are eternal enemies. The murderous Jews violate all agreements. I can't shake
hands with someone who I know is full of hatred towards me.

MAN ON THE STREET 3: No, the Jew is an enemy, how can I
shake my enemy's hand?

MAN ON THE STREET 4: I would not shake a Jew's hand. If I did
I would have to amputate it after.

Q: If a child ask[ed] you "who are the Jews?" what would you
answer?

MAN ON THE STREET 1: Allah's wrath is upon them and they all
stray from the path of righteousness. They are the filthiest people on the face of this earth because they care only about themselves: Not the Christians or the Muslims or any other religion.
The solution is clear, no only to me, but to everyone. If only the
Muslims declared Jihad we would see who stays home. We have
a few countries. . . . There is one country with a population of
over 60 to 70 million. If we let them only march, with no
weapons even, they would completely trample the Jews. They
would turn them into rotten carcasses under their feet. . . .[12]

*The following excerpt is from an interview with Professor Nizar
Riyan, a member of the Hamas political leadership in Gaza, courtesy of MEMRI:*

As for killing the resistance, I promise any Muslim who is listening
that the resistance will never be killed. A home from which a

mujahid was martyred all his brothers will set out [on Jihad]. By Allah, the fathers of the fighters, I swear...the fathers of the mujahideen who pass the age of fifty-five are begging us to give them guns so they can fight with us. The resistance is gaining strength and the number of mujahideen is growing. The killing of martyrs doesn't hurt us: They cannot hurt you beyond slight injury. Our martyrs are in heaven and this is our solace. On the other hand, their dead are in hell, as our Prophet said in battle of Uhud.[13]

Dr. Nawwal Nur and her son Hazem Saleh Abu Isma'il, Islamic preachers in the U.S., were interviewed by Iqra TV about the events of September 11. Below are some excerpts from the July 15, 2004, interview:

SHOW HOST: Did this horrible event, condemned by all the Muslims in the world, not change the image of Islam in the U.S.?

NAWWAL NUR: Not at all, it has not even been proved that Muslims committed it. There hasn't even been an investigation, there is nothing. They are confused about what happened. That is why they started to learn about Islam. Is it really possible that Islam would instigate such a thing? No, impossible. That is why more people converted to Islam.

HAZEM SALEH ABU ISMA'IL: I am one of those who believe these events were fabricated from the outset as a part of the global ground work for the distortion of Islam's image.[14]

Sheikh Abd Al-Aziz Al-Fawzan, a professor at Al-Imam University in Saudi Arabia, spoke about the duty of jihad on Saudi TV in November 2004:

Jihad is an individual duty applying to the Iraqi people. They need to wage this Jihad against this enemy until it leaves their country, especially as this enemy hurts their honor, blood, and property. Is it conceivable that we will let it be? Never. Jihad in this care is an individual duty applying to anyone capable of waging it in this country [15]

Muhammad Hassan, an Islamic cleric, spoke about child suicide bombers on Al-Majd TV on November 15, 2004:

Children, my brother, children teach the adults the meaning of manhood. Who would have thought that one day our children would make history... and blow themselves up? [16]

Saudi Cleric, Aed Al-Qarni, speaking on Iqra TV on December 26, 2004:

I pray to Allah that He will make the enemies fall into their own trap, and that he will destroy the Jews and their helpers from among the Christians and the Communists, and he will turn them into the Muslim spoils. I praise the Jihad, the sacrifice, and the resistance against the occupiers in Iraq. We curse them every night and pray that Allah will annihilate them, tear them apart, and grant us victory over them.... The Jihad in Falluja is a source of pride. It is astounding a city of 250,000 residents opposing a super power, by the standards of this world, downing their planes, destroying equipment, slaughtering them, taking hostage, and proclaiming "Allah Akhbar" from the mosques, and worshippers and their preacher cursing them in their prayers, and then come to others begging for forgiveness, and requesting a dialogue and ceasefire and negotiations. Who can say even one word against this true Jihad, against these colonialist occupiers?... Houses and young men must be sacrificed. Throats must be slit and skulls must be shattered. This is the path to victory to shahada and to sacrifice.[17]

Sheik Mahmoud Al-Masri spoke about September 11 on Al-Majd TV on a program that aired on March 2, 2005. Below are his words:

We were in America once, to preach for Allah. It was the time the WTC fell. It was an island called Queens, which is opposite Manhattan, where the WTC is located. Allah be praised, we were there for ten days or so, and Allah willed.... My friend, Allah protect him, said to me: "I'd love to see the two buildings since they're so beautiful." We looked at them from a distance, since the sea separated us from the buildings, and we said "how beautiful," because the beauty was indescribable. We went back home to sleep Allah be praised two or three hours later we had heard the two buildings had fallen. I said to my friend "Well done, doctor!" (Laughing.) He said to me: "We'll both be rewarded. We were a good omen." Allah be praised it was really difficult for five days, but from the crisis comes the gift of God. We thought we must show these Americans... these are wretched people. They need to know Islam, the Muslims, the value of the Prophet and his companions, and the value of the Muslims. We began to preach to them in classes on mercy and tolerance in Islam and so on. With Allah's grace, in the course of the seven days, 6,000 Americans converted to Islam, and declared Allah is the one and only God. Note the grace of Allah 6,000 Americans.... In the course of a single month an unimaginable number of 23,000 Americans converted to Islam.[18]

Saudi Cleric Aed Al Qarni also made these statements on February 7, 2005, on Channel 1 Saudi TV:

But we won't accept the Zionist rule or that of the White House, which is, in fact, a Black House. We say we have a religion, and we want to make the world understand this religion. We must rely on the divine source of authority in this matter, and not on what people understand, or on the declaration that "Whoever is not with us is against us." Whoever is not with Allah, His people, and His Messanger, is against goodness and virtue and truth.[19]

Below is a statement by Jordanian political science professor Ghazi Rabab'a on Al-Majd TV on May 22, 2005:

I want to finish with what the Prophet Muhammad said: "Judgment Day will not come until you fight the Jews, when you are east of the river and they are to its west, until the tree and the rock say 'Oh Muslim, oh servant of Allah, there is a Jew behind me, come and kill him.' Except for the Gharaqad tree which is the tree of the Jews." When this tradition was conveyed, 1400 years ago, there was not a single Jew in Palestine, nor was there a single Muslim east of the Jordan River. Nevertheless, this conflict is the fulfillment of the prophecy. The prophet Muhammad, who "does not speak of his own desire, foretold that we would clash with the Jews, and then the only dialogue would be a dialogue of weapons, to eradicate them from this land like the Crusaders before them."[20]

Saudi Cleric Muhammad Al-Munajjid said of Christian holidays on Al-Majd TV Saudi Arabia on January 1, 2005:

The problem is that the Christian holidays are accompanied by forbidden things, by immorality, abomination, adultery, alcohol, drunken dancing, and...revelry. They spend the entire night defying Allah. Haven't they learnt the lesson from what Allah wreaked upon the coast of Asia during the celebration of these forbidden holidays? At the height of immorality, Allah took vengeance on these criminals. Those celebrating spent what they called New Year's Eve in vacation resorts, pubs, and hotels. Allah struck them with an earth quake. He finished off the Richter scale all nine levels gone.[21]

Al Qaeda deputy commander Ayman al-Zawahiri misses no opportunity to exhort the terrorists in Iraq. Here are some of his statements:

On al Jazeera TV, August 4, 2005:

- "Our message is clear—what you saw in New York and Washington (in 2001) and what you are seeing in Afghanistan and Iraq, all these are nothing compared to what you will see next.
  "If you continue your politics against Muslims, you will see, God willing, such horror that you will forget the horrors of Vietnam."[22]

Al-Zawahiri Letter to Al-Zarqawi, July 9, 2005:

- "However, despite all of this, I say to you: that we are in a battle, and that more than half of this battle is taking place in the battlefield of the media. And that we are in a media battle in a race for the hearts and minds of our Umma. And that however far our capabilities reach, they will never be equal to one thousandth of the capabilities of the kingdom of Satan that is waging war on us. And we can kill the captives by bullet. That would achieve that which is sought after without exposing ourselves to the questions and answering to doubts. We don't need this."[23]

It's fair to ask: what effect does this have on the terrorists in Iraq? What are they willing to do when the hatemongers exhort them to terror? Who does the bidding of the hatemongers? Here is a MEMRI translation of an interview on April 20, 2005, with a terrorist captured in Iraq. Warning: This is very graphic, and not for the faint of heart:

Captured Iraqi Terrorist 'Adnan Elias: We Beheaded a Policeman, Filled His Corpse with TNT, and Used It to Blow Up Others

'ADNAN ELIAS: We tied (the policeman) up and blindfolded him, and then threw him into the trunk. Then we went to the house of the Emir. We untied his hands and eyes, and then punished him.

INTERVIEWER: How did you punish him?

'ADNAN ELIAS: We whipped him.

INTERVIEWER: You whipped him?

'ADNAN ELIAS: Yes, Muhsin did.

INTERVIEWER: And you?

'ADNAN ELIAS: I didn't whip him. I just stood there holding the gun.

INTERVIEWER: Go on.

'ADNAN ELIAS: They told us to take him to the house of Habib 'Izzat Hamu. We took him out there. We said to him: "Why did you do this and that . . . . Why are you after us?" He answered:

"It's out of our hands. We get orders." Then we were told to bring a knife.

INTERVIEWER: You slaughtered him?

'ADNAN ELIAS: Yes, sir. Habib 'Izzat Hamu got the knife. He slaughtered him, and when he was dead, he opened his shirt buttons and cut open his stomach.

INTERVIEWER: Who opened him up?

'ADNAN ELIAS: Muhsin, sir.

INTERVIEWER: When a doctor performs an operation he wears a surgeon's mask over his nose and mouth.

'ADNAN ELIAS: No sir, he didn't wear one.

INTERVIEWER: He didn't wear one?

'ADNAN ELIAS: No sir, he didn't wear one. He cut open his stomach and took stuff out.

INTERVIEWER: What did he take out?

'ADNAN ELIAS: I don't know, his guts.

INTERVIEWER: Weren't you nauseous? Didn't you vomit?

'ADNAN ELIAS: You mean Muhsin?

INTERVIEWER: No, you.

'ADNAN ELIAS: I was standing a little bit aside.

INTERVIEWER: And he didn't vomit or get nauseous?

'ADNAN ELIAS: No, sir.

INTERVIEWER: What is he, Dracula?

'ADNAN ELIAS: Huh?

INTERVIEWER: Go on.

'ADNAN ELIAS: Yes, sir. He opened him up, took stuff out, and put TNT and explosives inside. Then he sewed up his stomach with thick thread.

INTERVIEWER: With thread?

'ADNAN ELIAS: Yes. And a needle. He put the buttons back in place...

INTERVIEWER: He buttoned him up.

'ADNAN ELIAS: Yes, he buttoned him up. We were told to take him in the car near the square in Tel A'far. We threw him there and placed his head back on his shoulders.

INTERVIEWER: My God!

'ADNAN ELIAS: Fifteen to thirty minutes later they told his family to come and get their son. His father came with two policemen. They picked up the body and made no more than two steps—we were standing far away—Ahmad Sinjar pressed the button.

INTERVIEWER: By remote control.

'ADNAN ELIAS: The body exploded on them, and they died.

INTERVIEWER: So his father and the two policemen died.

'ADNAN ELIAS: Yes sir, and we took off.[24]

FIVE

Iran: The Central Terrorist Nation, Long before September 11

Iran has been at war with the United States since it seized our embassy in Tehran in 1979 and held sixty-two Americans hostage for 444 days. In the Clinton era, we were led to believe that the Iranians had become "moderates" and that unlike the regime under its founder, Ayatollah Ruhollah Khomeni, we could deal with the new ayatollahs diplomatically.

The chief Iranian "moderate" was Ayatollah Rafsangani, their president at the time. We heard little about Rafsangani and how he regarded America. Here are some statements he made in an interview with Al-Hayat (an Arabic newspaper) in 2001, before September 11. It has been translated by the indispensable people of MEMRI:

The Reformist's Victory

According to Rafsangani, the most notable accomplishment of the recent presidential election is the large turnout of the Iranian people, rather than the re-election of President Khatami.

Relations with the U.S.

Rafsangani stated that Iran does not distinguish between a Republican or a Democratic administration in the U.S. and stressed [that], **"restoring relations with the U.S. depends on a change in American policy towards Iran ... the U.S. has to endorse an acceptable policy towards Palestine, and to stop [American] support of Israel."**

Rafsangani said that during his term as president, he insisted the U.S. thaw Iranian assets in the U.S. as a precondition to resumption of negotiations with the U.S., while Khatami has not posed this as a precondition, but rather sufficed with a call for a change in America's policy towards Iran. He stated that the steps America has taken so far in the field of commerce towards Iran are "minute, partial, and have no meaning or effect."

Rafsangani defined American military presence in the region as "a humiliation to the region's peoples" and despite the fact that these [U.S.] forces are not present on Iranian soil, "we consider our neighbors, the Arab countries, as equal to us in this respect."

Israel

Rafsangani criticized the election of Ariel Sharon: "Even if we refrain from claiming that the election of Sharon is an act of insanity, it can be admitted that such a step is irrational...."

Rafsangani warned, "If the Zionists wish to take irrational actions, they will face a serious and immediate response, at first from within Palestine, and then from neighboring Islamic countries."

Rafsangani added: "The reactions will not be limited to the Zionists alone, for the Israelis do not take such steps before [receiving] the go-ahead from the Americans. Therefore, if such [steps] are taken, the United States will also be held responsible, [and then] one cannot expect a limited area of conflict.... [Iran] will not stay idle but rather respond with force."

Assistance to the Palestinians

Rafsangani stressed, "We shall not confine [our] assistance to the Palestinian problem, because we perceive it as our problem ... starting from financial aid, through media and political assistance at the international level, and if the need arises, we will not withhold military assistance."[1]

Moderation in Iran is now, and has been since 1979, a façade. The Iranians are a very capable adversary. They have adapted to the new means of fighting wars—television, the Internet, and more— better than the rest of the terrorist world. With the vast majority of their population under age thirty and with the proliferation of televised media, they are working hard to make the world believe that they are not only moderates, but Westernized. In truth, they are neither. They are, as they have been since they overthrew the Shah twenty-eight years ago, the most radical and dedicated terrorist regime in the world.

If Iranian Supreme Leader Ayatollah Ali Khamenei has a sense of humor, he probably chuckles himself to sleep at night. Khamenei must be amazed at America's policy—or lack of one—to deal with the enormous threat his nation poses to us and the entire non-Shiite world. According to many statements by Secretary of State Rice, our policy toward Iran is one of isolating it, by diplomacy and UN Security Council "sanction" resolutions from the world community.

So far, Iran is so isolated that: (1) Russia is openly building and supplying Iran's nuclear program, and has supplied Iran with sophisticated anti-aircraft missile systems that essentially preclude air strikes against the nuclear sites by all except stealth aircraft or missiles; (2) China is trading arms and technology to Iran for oil; and (3) Venezuela's Hugo Chavez has allied his nation with Iran (and China) in hopes of gaining weapons and technology and constricting American access to oil. At this rate, isolation could soon land Iranian president Mahmoud Ahmadinejad a seat on the New York Stock Exchange.

To the isolation policy and the UN, Ahmadinejad answers regularly with a Bronx cheer. The Iranian terrorist regime—the central terrorist sponsor in the world—has managed to place Ahmadinejad, Iran's "president," on the world stage as the face of the theocracy. Ahmadinejad puts a smiling, young face on the kakistocracy of the ayatollahs. Instead of a fulminating, beturbaned, bearded face out of the twelfth century, the world sees a modern, fit, youngish man proclaiming the inevitability of a new Islamic caliphate to rule the world. He tries to rally young Iranians (mostly unsuccessfully) but has captured the media's attention as an Izod-wearing Westernized face of the most radical of all Islamofascist regimes. It is important that we pay attention to Ahmadinejad, the Izod Ayatollah—who speaks the words the real ayatollahs approve—but even more so that we listen, carefully, to Khamenei.

Iran has been at war with the United States since the ayatollahs seized control in 1979. It created and sponsors Hizballah, the terrorist organization that has more American blood on its hands than any other except al Qaeda. In 1979, the Iranians seized the American embassy in Tehran and kept our diplomatic staff prisoner for 444 days, releasing them on the day Ronald Reagan was inaugurated.

They were responsible for the Hizballah bombing of the Marine barracks in Beirut in 1983, which killed 241 Marines and sailors.

At this writing, and at least since 2005, Iran has been manufacturing and smuggling into Iraq the deadliest form of improvised explosive device: the so-called "EFP" or "explosively formed penetrator." This very sophisticated weapon is mislabeled "improvised." It is a finely machined and well-designed mine. Its main features are two: a "shaped charge" explosive, which directs the explosive force to first compress and propel at hypersonic speed the second, a metal rod so highly compressed and moving so fast that it penetrates the armor of even American M1-A1 main battle tanks.

When I visited Baghdad in December 2005, a senior American general told me about the EFPs and said that they were responsible for more American deaths than any other weapon the insurgents were using. That remains true today.

We know Iran is killing Americans daily. And yet, we fail to listen carefully to the words of its leaders.

The following is an excerpt from a speech made by the Grand Leader of the Islamic Republic of Iran Ayatollah Sayyid Ali Khamenei in a meeting with thousands of high school students from throughout the country on March 14, 2005. The participants at the meeting were members of student Islamic associations.

You can see that some twenty-six years after the revolution, the Iranian people still chant the slogan of "death to America." This is because they know that if they become neglectful of the plots being hatched against them by the global arrogance, they will surely suffer from those plots.

In fact, the "death to America" that is chanted by our people is similar to the phrase "I seek the protection of Allah against the cursed Satan," which is recited at the beginning of each Qur'anic chapter before "In the Name of Allah, the Compassionate, the Merciful." What is the reason for seeking the protection of Allah from the cursed Satan? It is for the believers not to forget the presence of the Satan, not to forget even for a single moment that the Satan is ready to attack them and destroy the spiritual fortifications that protect their belief.

In the same manner, "death to America" is also meant for the Iranian nation not to forget that the world's hegemonic powers who formerly had great interests in this country and who lost those interests because of the Islamic Revolution are always trying to once again secure those interests and increase their wealth at the cost of hindering our country's progress and destroying the bright prospects of our talented youngsters.[2]

Khamenei's Message to Hajj Pilgrims on January 26, 2005:

At present, the Islamic world is faced with an all-out siege, both on the economic and the technological fronts, as well as with a propaganda offensive, and most recently with military occupation. The occupation of Palestine and the holy city of Quds [Jerusalem] have culminated in the occupation of Iraq and Afghanistan. The Zionist octopus—along with the vicious and despicable U.S. imperialism— now harbors plans for the entire region of the Middle East, as well as North Africa and the entire Islamic world. They have created the general awakening, which has breathed new life into the Islamic nation [Ummah], the target of their vengeance and spite.

The U.S. and the Western imperialists have finally concluded that Muslim countries and nations, especially those of the Middle East, form the core of this awakening and resistance to their plans for global domination. They foresee that if they fail to control or suppress this Islamic awakening in the next few years with political and economic measures, through propaganda, and as a last resort through military aggression, all their plans for absolute global hegemony and control of the most vital oil and gas resources, which constitute the sole powerhouse of their industrial machinery and [the sole] cause of their material edge over the rest of humanity, will come to nothing.

If that happens, the big Western and Zionist capitalists, who are the real backstage players in all imperialist governments, will fall from the height of their power and their domination over the nations.

Imperialist arrogance has deployed all its capabilities to this end. It has launched this fateful war, using political pressure on one front, threats of economic sanctions on another, and employing propaganda tactics in one place and bombs, missiles, tanks, and troops in other places, such as Iraq and Afghanistan, just as it did before in Palestine and Quds.

The most important tool of these predatory savages is the deceptive mask of hypocrisy that they wear. They equip and dispatch their assassination squads to murder innocent people and talk of waging war on terrorism. They openly support the bloodthirsty terrorist regime that has usurped Palestine, and label as terrorists the defenders of Palestine, who strive with their backs to the wall.

They manufacture, supply, and use nuclear, chemical, and biological weapons of mass destruction. They have perpetrated such horrors as Hiroshima and Halabja, and on the Iranian warfront during the imposed war, while they profess to be against the proliferation of weapons of mass destruction.

They themselves are behind the dirty drug trade mafia, but claim to be fighting the narcotics trade. They make a display of supporting science and the globalization of science, and yet obstruct the development of science and technology in the Islamic world, considering the emergence of nuclear technology for peaceful purposes in Islamic countries a moral sin. They talk of freedom and the rights of minorities while depriving Muslim girls of the right to education for the sin of wearing the Islamic scarf. They speak glibly about the freedom of expression and belief, while counting every expression of opinion about Zionism as a crime.

They ban the publication of many outstanding Islamic works and forbid in the U.S. even the publication of the documents retrieved from the U.S. spy den in Tehran. They rant about human rights while setting up scores of torture centers—such as the ones at Guantanamo and Abu Ghraib—or maintain a conniving silence about such incredible outrages.

They talk about respect for all religions, while extending their support to such renegades as Salman Rushdie, who has been sentenced to capital punishment, and the BBC, which broadcasts sacrilegious statements against Islamic sanctities.

However, as a consequence of the insolent and foolishly reckless conduct of the U.S. and British rulers, this mask of deception and hypocrisy has been fractured. With their own hands, they have stuffed the hearts of Muslim nations and youth with hatred for the arrogant imperialists. Should free elections be held today in any Muslim country, the people would definitely vote against the wishes of the U.S. and Britain.

Excerpt from Supreme Leader's Speech to government officials on the Eid-al-Fitr, November 4, 2005:

It is a grave mistake if one holds the view that the Islamic governments' backing off in the face of arrogant powers on the issue of Palestine will appease these powers. As a matter of fact, the frequent backing off on the part of Islamic governments has prompted the arrogant U.S. government to nurture the vain dream of dominating the Middle East.

The United States is dreaming of a region totally under its influence and domination, but today the reality on the ground is something else. The silence of Islamic governments and their passivity on the political and international scene will make arrogant powers, especially U.S. administration, even more impudent and insolent.[3]

MEMRI TV DVD, Iranian Friday Sermons, April 26, 2006:

Look how the arrogant people of the world become enraged. The things uttered by people like Bush and his circle show that they are becoming enraged. This is because you are now making progress with full force. Our enemies and the evil global arrogance the West have realized that they cannot embark upon a military campaign against the Iranian people and the Islamic Republic of Iran, because this would cause them great losses. This is true and they have understood this correctly. **The Americans should know if they take any aggressive action against the Islamic Iran, Iran will harm their interest wherever possible in the world.** (Chanting: "Death to America, Death to America") We are not the kind of people to sit and wait for somebody to strike at us, without striking back. We are people of peace and tranquility. We do not attack anybody. The reason is obvious. What country did we ever attack? Against what

country did we ever start a war? What country did we ever
threaten? We are not the kind of people who do such things? But
we are the kind of people that when attacked by anybody, we
strike back twice as hard. (Chanting: "Allah Akbar—Khamene'i is
the leader, Death to those who reject the rude of the Jurisprudent,
Death to America, Death to Israel, Death to the hypocrites and
Saddam.")[4]

MEMRI TV DVD, Iranian Friday Sermon, March 21, 2006:

We have enemies. These enemies do not like our people to move
forward. These enemies are lead by the regime of the United
States of America.... (Chanting "Death to America") Today the
world hates the methods of America. Today, in the Islamic world,
from Indonesia to Morocco.... Anywhere you go and ask people
they harbor hatred towards the leaders of the White House deep
in their hearts....

They accuse the Islamic Republic of violating human rights.
This is one of the funny jokes of our time. America has become
the standard-bearer of human rights. Which America? The America of Hiroshima, the America of Guantanamo, the America of
Abu Ghraib, the America that generates wars and insecurity
through out the world. They say we are violating human rights,
They themselves are the greatest violators of human rights.

If in the world today.... I don't mean only the Islamic world. If
a referendum was held throughout the world, you should have no
doubt that the current American president would be grouped
together with Sharon, Saddam, and Milosevic, as the icons of evil.
Today America poses a threat to peace and security in the world.
Therefore the slogan "Death to America" is no longer used by only

our people. Today you see through out the world people setting fire to the effigy of the American president and chanting the slogan "Death to America." This is because of the American regimes exaggerated demands, its arrogance, its vanity and its desire to control.

Source: Voice of the Islamic Republic of Iran, Tehran, September 18, 2006

Iranian Leader Ayatollah Ali Khamenei—Broadcast by Iranian radio (Regarding the Pope's remarks at Regensburg University):

KHAMEINEI: They have to create crises in order to be able to pursue their wicked intentions in the international community. This is the issue. This is what I'm worried about, [what lies] behind these remarks: mistrust between Muslims and Christians, vindictiveness between Christian and Muslim nations, painting an ugly image of Muslims, especially in those countries in which they are minorities, such as European countries, such as America, the creation of pretexts for the repression of Muslim communities in those countries on the baseless charge of terrorism and the like. It is policies like these that lie behind this affair. We must pay attention to this.

A few years ago a European leader in a meeting with me talked about a war between Christians and Muslims. I was surprised and asked whether there was going to be a war between Christians and Muslims. I told him that Muslims do not have any motivation to fight the Christians. And that in more than a hundred years, all major wars in the world including the two world wars and the Franco-German wars were between Christians. I was wondering why he had said that. After sometime, the Twin Towers incident took place in New York and the U.S. president commented that a Crusade had started. The person who had talked to me was one of those who was later directly involved in the American-Zionist project of attacking Iraq. Then I realized that what he had told me was based on an agreement among the heads of the world's arrogant powers. That is those who had formed a circle of American-Zionist conspiracies against the Middle East. Their first step was to attack Iraq. Then the meaning of that man's words became clear to me: A Crusade, a war between Christians and Muslims.

Of course they did not succeed. Since then they have made many efforts.... Unfortunately this time it has been said by the Pope, a Christian cleric.... But it is surprising to hear this from a clergy. It is regrettable that a senior clerical official in the Christian world becomes a tool for what the arrogant powers' politicians and power brokers and the plunderers of national wealth and those who create crises. It is very regrettable. Muslims should pay attention to this. Those who take stances vis-à-vis these unfair remarks should note the direction of their attack and movement. The one who benefits from such moves is not the Pope and the likes of Pope. The world powers and the Zionists and America are the ones [who benefits from this move]. It is the great Satan that is playing a part behind the scene. [Chants: "Death to America"]

May God lead us to the right path and help us carry out our tasks with knowledge, awareness and endeavour. God willing, we will entrap the enemies of Islam with their own plots." [Chants: "Oh Khamenei, we are all ready for your command."]

Ali Khamenei, aired on the Iranian News Channel on June 4, 2006:

ALI KHAMENEI: In an attempt to threaten Iran, you claim you can guarantee the flow of energy in this region. You are wrong. If

you make the slightest mistake regarding Iran, the flow of
energy in this region will surely be jeopardized seriously. You
must know this.

CROWD: Allah Akbar. Allah Akbar. Allah Akbar. Khamenei is the
leader. Death to those who reject the rule of the Jurisprudent.
Death to America. Death to England. Death to the hypocrites
[Mojahedin-e Khalq] and Saddam. Death to Israel.

ALI KHAMENEI: You will never be able to guarantee the safe supply of energy in this region.

We adhere to our ambitions and to our national interests.
Whoever threatens our interests will feel the sharp wrath of
this people.

CROWD: Allah Akbar. Allah Akbar. Allah Akbar. Khamenei is the
leader. Death to those who reject the rule of the Jurisprudent.
Death to America. Death to England. Death to the hypocrites
[Mojahedin-e Khalq] and Saddam. Death to Israel.[5]

There is more, much more, from the ayatollas and from Ahmadine-
jad himself:

Following are excerpts from a Friday sermon at Tehran Univer-
sity, delivered by Ayatollah Ahmad Jannati, Secretary of the
Guardian Council. The sermon was aired on Channel 1, Iranian TV
on February 17, 2006:

AYATOLLAH AHMAD JANNATI: Western culture and civilization—
and especially criminal America—are heading towards a serious collapse.

CROWD: Allah Akbar.
Allah Akbar.
Allah Akbar.
Khamenei is the leader.

Death to those who reject the rule of the Jurisprudent.

Death to America.

Death to England.

Death to the hypocrites [Mojahedin-e Khalq] and Saddam.

Death to Israel.

AYATOLLAH AHMAD JANNATI: You have made homosexuality official and legal. I spit in your face. The world should be
ashamed of your deeds. Humanity should be ashamed. Your
shamelessness should cause humanity to sweat in shame. A
boy marrying a boy. . . .

People are prepared to sacrifice their lives for the sake of
the Prophet. There is no doubt about it. We've sacrificed so
many martyrs. You insult him. . . .

CROWD: Death to America.[6]

Channel 1, Iranian TV, July 15, 2005:

The last issue I will discuss is the explosions in London. In my
opinion, the Americans, Israelis, and Europeans should be
ashamed and their brow should be covered in sweat because they
cannot find the answer to these events. They say one possibility is
that it was al Qaeda. But al Qaeda means Bush and Blair. Who
established al Qaeda? You are the ones who should be put on trial.
You were the mother of al Qaeda. You are the ones who gave birth
to this illegitimate child. Who are you complaining about? This is
one possibility. The other possibility is that the English government itself caused this situation. This possibility was also raised
regarding September 11—that the Americans themselves caused
it. This because they have the most to gain from these events. If
we want to see who caused these events, we need to see who has

the most to gain. [O]n September 11 it was the Americans who had the most to gain. Here too the Americans and the English are trying to rake in the most of the profits.[7]

Channel 1, Iranian TV, June 25, 2004:

Anyone who confronted the revolution . . . eventually collapsed, or is about to collapse. America is the last one and Allah willing, it will also collapse, and so will Israel. In Iraq there are many problems. May Allah, by virtue of the Hidden Imam, remove the evil America and Israel from humanity

Channel 1, Iranian TV, June 4, 2004:

Why do the Muslims remain silent? The day will come and they too will get involved because of their silence. What consequences will this bring them? In Palestine this kind of disaster has come and still comes upon the Muslims and you remained polite. You kept silent, held conventions, condemned, acted ceremoniously, and got up and left. This situation developed in Iraq. If the situation in Iraq continues as it does in Israel, tomorrow they will come to Egypt. Tomorrow they will come to Algeria. All the Arab countries and the non Arab countries will be their targets.

They will continue the line of swallowing the world. We are no longer speaking of geographic borders but of swallowing the world. **Therefore every Muslim and every honorable man who is not a Muslim must stand against the Americans, English, and Israelis and endanger their interests wherever they may be. (Chanting: "Allah Akbar, Death to America.") They must not have security.** If Muslims have no security neither must they. They are the people of "Dar-Al-Harb," so why should they have security? I say to my Iraqi brothers and sisters, Oh brother and sister, resist, stand fast. . . . All of you gather under one flag. When you see the source of emulation Ayatollah Sistani, God save him, standing strong and stead fast full of the fear of God and wisdom. In any case he is out there. Others must not stand against him. He must be accepted as a religious source of authority. Anyhow, religion is your savior. Without religion you will not be saved. You will be massacred and for no reason. (Chanting: "Islam is victorious. America will be annihilated.")[8]

Mahmoud Ahmadinejad, president of Iran, has been identified by some as a participant in the 1979 embassy hostage-taking. He is the most visible of the Iranian leaders. His is the "modern" face of the terrorist regime. Ahmadinejad jokes with CBS correspondent Mike Wallace, appears in what Americans call "business casual" attire, not the robes of an ayatollah. He even has a blog (www.ahmadinejad.ir) on which he—or someone—posts messages to the American people, even to mothers of American soldiers in Iraq.

He may have convinced some that he is the real power in Iran, but Ahmadinejad is the Iranian version of The Great Oz: don't look at those men behind the curtain. They are Supreme Leader Khamenei and his eighty-six-member "Assembly of Experts"—all Shiite religious "scholars" whose job it is to keep Iran on the terrorist path. Beneath them is the "Expediency Council," which has at least forty members and debates policy delegated by the Assembly of Experts. There are more, but all have one thing in common: they are religious or pseudo-religious figures. Ahmadinejad is the secular face of radical Shia Islam, an "Izod ayatollah."

*We cannot ignore Ahmadinejad. His words are those of the aya-
tollahs, filtered through a lens of golf clothes and smiles to the
media. He is, like the ayatollahs, bent on dominating the Middle
East and more. Here are just a few of his statements:*

- **Undoubtedly, I say that this slogan and goal is achiev-
  able, and with the support and power of God, we will
  soon experience a world without the United States
  and Zionism and will breathe in the brilliant time of
  Islamic sovereignty over today's world.**[9]
- Such people are using words like "it's not possible." They say
  how could we have a world without America and Zionism? But
  you know well that this slogan and goal can be achieved and
  can definitely be realized.[10]
- In his struggle against the World Arrogance, our dear Imam
  targeted the central and command base of the enemy, namely
  the occupying regime in Al-Quds. I have no doubt that the
  new wave that has started in dear Palestine and which we witness today all over the Islamic world will soon wipe this
  scourge of shame from the Islamic world. This can be done.

  We have to watch out for conspiracies. For more than fifty
  years, the World Arrogance has tried to give recognition to the
  existence of this fake regime [Israel] and they have made many
  efforts to first stabilize it and then take further steps.

  Some twenty-seven or twenty-eight years ago, they took an
  important step in this regard and, unfortunately, one of the
  front-line countries made this mistake, and we hope that
  country [Egypt] will rectify its mistake.

  Recently, a new conspiracy has been plotted and is under-
  way. They have been forced to evacuate a corner of Palestine

and this was imposed on them by the Palestinian nation. But they want to sell this as the final victory and use the evacuation of Gaza and the creation of a Palestinian state as an excuse to end the Palestinian cause and goal.

Today they are making an evil and deceptive effort to turn the struggle into an internal conflict of the Islamic world. They want to create conflict among Palestinian groups inside Palestine by making them greedy for political positions or high office, so that these groups abandon the decisive issue of Palestine and turn on each other.

With the excuse of having cleared the Gaza Strip to show their good will, they want a group of Muslim nations to recognize this corrupt regime, and I am very hopeful and pray to God that the Palestinian nation and the dear Palestinian groups will be cautious of such sedition. . . .

If we put it behind us successfully, God willing, it will pave the way for the annihilation of the Zionist regime and it will be a downhill route.

I warn all the leaders in the Islamic world to beware of this conspiracy. If any of them takes a step towards the recognition of this regime [Israel], then he will burn in the fire of the Islamic umma (nation) and will have eternal shame stamped on his forehead, regardless of whether he did this under pressure by the dominant powers, or lack of understanding or naiveté or selfishness or worldly incentives.

The issue of Palestine is the issue of the Islamic world. Those who are closeted behind closed doors cannot make decisions on this issue and the Islamic nation does not allow this historical enemy to exist at the heart of the Islamic world.[11]

In a December 14, 2005, speech Ahmadinejad gave in the city of Zahedan, carried live on Iranian television, he reportedly made the following comments:

If the Europeans are telling the truth in their claim that they have killed six million Jews in the Holocaust during the World War II—which seems they are right in their claim because they insist on it and arrest and imprison those who oppose it, why should the Palestinian nation pay for the crime. Why have they come to the very heart of the Islamic world and are committing crimes against the dear Palestine using their bombs, rockets, missiles and sanctions.... The same European countries have imposed the illegally established Zionist regime on the oppressed nation of Palestine. If you have committed the crimes so give a piece of your land somewhere in Europe or America and Canada or Alaska to them to set up their own state there.... Then the Iranian nation will have no objections, will stage no rallies on the Qods Day and will support your decision.[12]

The following statements by Ahmadinejad were aired on Islamic Republic of Iran News Network Television (IRINN) in 2006:

- June 21, 2006: Open your eyes and see the fate of Pharaoh.... Open your eyes and see what happened to the Portuguese Empire. See the final fate of the British Empire.... I am telling you [major powers], if you do not abandon the path of falsehood and return to the path of justice, your doomed destiny will be annihilation, misfortune, and abjectness.
- July 11, 2006: The anger of Muslims may reach an explosion point soon. If such a day comes, they [Western governments] should know that the waves of the blast will not remain within

the boundaries of our region and will engulf the corrupt powers that support this fake regime too.

■ August 15, 2006: And you, for your part, if you would like to
have good relations with the Iranian nation in the future, recognize the Iranian nation's right. Recognize the Iranian
nation's greatness. **And bow down before the greatness of
the Iranian nation and surrender.** If you don't accept [to
do this], the Iranian nation will later force you to surrender
and bow down.[13]

■ In December 2005, CNN reported that the president of Iran
made the following public declaration:

They have invented a myth that Jews were massacred and
place this above God, religions, and the prophets. The West has
given more significance to the myth of the genocide of the
Jews, even more significant than God, religion, and the
prophets, (it) deals very severely with those who deny this myth
but does not do anything to those who deny God, religion, and
the prophet. If you have burned the Jews, why don't you give a
piece of Europe, the United States, Canada or Alaska to Israel?
Our question is, if you have committed this huge crime, why
should the innocent nation of Palestine pay for this crime?[14]

In 2006, Ahmadinejad gave a speech for the twenty-seventh
anniversary of the Islamic Revolution in which he said: "Now in the
West insulting the prophet is allowed, but questioning the Holocaust is considered a crime.... We ask, why do you insult the
prophet? The response is that it is a matter of freedom, while in fact
they (who insult the founder of Islam) are hostages of the Zionists.
**And the people of the U.S. and Europe should pay a heavy
price for becoming hostages to Zionists.**"[15]

The excerpts below are from MEMRI video translations:

May 24, 2006, Iranian News Channel

Despite the political pressure, the conspiracies, and the use of international organizations by the enemies, they have not suc-ceeded in preventing the Iranian people from obtaining nuclear energy. Today they have come up with a conspiracy. Today they want to generate dispute, division, and despair, thus preventing the Iranian people from realizing all its rights. They know that from the outside, they cannot harm the Iranian people in the slightest. They know that any transgression, or the mere thought of violating the rights of the Iranian people will be met with a slap of eternal and historic proportions by the Iranian people and the youth of Khorramshahr. This is the cry of the Khorramsharhr. They are shouting in defense of nuclear energy. They are insisting on the indisputable right of the Iranian people to benefit from nuclear energy. Listen to the slogan of the people of Khor-ramshahr: (Chanting: "**Nuclear energy is our indisputable right**. In spirit and in blood we will redeem you, oh Mahmoud.")[16]

Jaam-e Jam 2 TV (Iran), February 11, 2006:

The affront to the honor of the Prophet of Islam is in fact an affront to the worship of God, and to the seeking of truth and jus-tice, and an affront to all the prophets of God. Obviously, all those who harm the honor of the prophet of Islam.... (Chanting: "Death to Denmark, Death to Denmark.") As a representative of the great Iranian people, I call upon the free people of the world, Christians and Jews, to rise together with the Muslims and not let a handful of shameless Zionists, who have been defeated in Palestine, to harm the sanctity of the prophets. I call upon them to not let a few weak governments—which owe their rise in power to the support of the Zionists—support them in this ugly manner.

As I have said before as far as several aggressive European governments are concerned, as far as the great Satan the U.S. is concerned, it is permissible to harm the honor of the divine prophets but it is a crime to ask questions about the myth of the Holocaust, and about how the false regime occupying Palestine came into being. On the basis of this myth the pillaging Zionist regime has managed for sixty years to extort all Western governments and to justify its crimes in the occupied lands, killing women and children, demolishing homes and turning defenseless people into refugees.

When we protest to the Europeans, they say there is freedom in our country, They are lying when they claim they have freedom. They are hostages in the hands of the Zionists. The people of Europe and America are the ones that should be paying the heavy price of this hostage taking. How come one is allowed to harm the honor of the prophets in your country, but is forbidden to research the myth of the Holocaust. You are a bunch of tyrants, who are dependent upon the Zionists and who are held hostage by them.

We propose the following: If you are not lying, allow a group of neutral, honest, researchers to come to Europe, and talk to the people, examine documents, and let people know the findings of their research about the Holocaust myth. You have prevented you own scholars from researching this issue. They are allowed to study anything except the Holocaust myth. Are these not medieval methods?

Even today, a group of people convene and declare: "We rule that the Holocaust happened and everybody must think the same." This is a medieval way of thinking. On the face of it, the technology has changed, but the culture and the way of thinking remain medieval. If you are looking for the real Holocaust, you should look for it in Palestine. Over there the pillaging Zionists are massacring the Palestinian people everyday.

If you are looking for the holocaust you should find then among the oppressed in Iraq. Today all the people throughout the world are familiar with your methods of thinking. Your behavior is the essence of Western liberalism.[17]

The following are excerpts from an address delivered by Iranian president Mahmoud Ahmadinejad, which aired on Jaam-e Jam 1 TV on October 20, 2006:

MAHMOUD AHMADINEJAD: This [Zionist regime] was established in order to swallow up the entire region, and to place it at the disposal of the world forces. It is a big lie that it was done in order to protect those killed in World War II, and in order to compensate them.

Over 60 million people were killed in World War II. Let's assume you are right, and six million [Jews] were among those killed. How come none of you mourn the other 54 million? Why don't you pay reparations to them? Why don't you ever think about them? All your sorrow, your pity, your mourning cries are over [victims] who were counted by I don't know whom. . . .

. . . .The existence of this regime is so essential for these countries that in some of them, they even built monuments. You know that every country builds monuments for the objects of their pride. They take their children, from an early age, to show them these monuments, in order to help them develop their identity, and to instill in their memory the things that make them proud, in order to feel power and honor. In some of these countries, they set up monuments whose purpose was to degrade that very nation. From an early age, they take their children and say to them: "Look, our ancestors were murderers. Our ancestors used to burn people. We are in debt."

. . . .Why does America extort the world, under the pretext of the Holocaust? Why does England extort [the world]? Wasn't it England that laid the foundations for the fear that led the Jews to flee to the occupied lands?

They said: "We want to establish a place for the survivors." How many survivors were there? With false promises, you gathered the wretched people from Africa, South America, Asia, and North America, and you brought them there. You banished one people from its land, and you want to create another people by force. Why? Why? Are all those now living in Palestine survivors of the war? We asked [these Westerners]: "The current leader of the Zionist regime—where did his parents live? Where were they?" As you know, some of the leaders of the Zionist regime are in fact Iranians.

The life of this regime depended on military threat, military force, and the legend that it was invincible. Today, with God's grace, this false legend has collapsed, with the help of the young believers of Palestine, and thanks to the believing, self-sacrificing commanders of Hizballah. Today, the Zionists do not feel secure even in their own homes, anywhere in the world.

Today, this community, which was gathered by force, and under false pretexts, and whose members were joined to one another by a paperclip, in order to create a false illusion of a nation. . . . Today, they have fallen apart. I declare here, loud and clear: With God's grace, this regime has lost the philosophy of its existence.

I said to them: If you do not agree, open the doors, open the gates, and allow these uninvited guests to return to their countries. Let them return to their homeland. If the Western countries that support the Zionists feel sympathetic toward them, they should give them financial aid, so that they can live in their own countries.

We have some advice for the supporters of this regime. We say to them: First of all, do not seek a new crime. Every crime being perpetrated today, every youth who dies in Palestine today, every home that is demolished, and every incursion into the neighboring countries will be accredited to the supporters of this regime, and the nations will exact their revenge.

Our proposal is as follows: Since you brought [this regime] over there, you yourselves pick it up, by the arms and legs, and remove it from there. This will make the peoples of the region improve their attitude toward you. These will be the first steps to a long-lasting friendship with the peoples of the region. This will be to your advantage.

You may say: "We feel uncomfortable doing this, because the Zionists control our countries, the propaganda machinery is at their disposal, and if we want to gain voters, we need their money and their support. Therefore, we feel uncomfortable doing this."

Fine. We made you another proposal: Allow that which you advocate take place in Palestine. After all, you advocate democracy, and you claim that the peoples should control their own destiny. So let the Palestinian people decide upon its own path by means of a referendum. In response, you say: "We might lose our reputation." Our response is: You have no reputation left anyway! Where do you still have a reputation anywhere in the world?....

This [Zionist] regime is on the verge of death, and we advise you to start thinking about your long-term interests and long-term relations with the peoples of the region. At the end of the day, these are all ultimatums. No one should complain tomorrow. The things are stated clearly.

What is this Security Council anyway? **The whole world knows that America and England are the enemies of the Iranian nation.**

CROWD: Allah Akbar.

Allah Akbar.

Khamenei is the leader.

Death to those who oppose the rule of the jurisprudent

Death to America

Death to England

Death to the hypocrites and Saddam

Death to Israel.

AHMADINEJAD: They have taken control of the leading positions in the Security Council, and have the right of veto, and they are prosecuting and judging us, and they want to carry out the verdict. Sir, this is the logic of pharaonic times. The days of this logic are over. **The Security Council, in its present condition, is illegitimate. Its resolutions are illegitimate.** Do you want to be the judges, the rulers, the prosecutors, and those who carry out the verdicts? These days are over. Nobody accepts this behavior of yours. Even the illiterate old women of the Himalayas will not accept this behavior of yours.[18]

Ahmadinejad is not the power in Iran, but he speaks for them. We cannot ignore his words, or theirs. We get few glimpses of the other powerful figures behind Ahmadinejad. Those we see should be examined closely.

Ayatollah Mohammad Emami Kashani—apparently a member of Iran's "Supreme National Security Council"—spoke to the Iranian News Agency on June 16, 2006. He denies Hizballah is a terrorist organization and maintains the party line that Iran's nuclear program is peaceful. Here is the IRNA report:

A senior cleric on Friday dismissed hues and cries by certain states, led by the U.S. and Israel, against Iran's peaceful nuclear program and against its SCO observer state membership, saying the claims are "foams and bubbles" caused by the U.S. and its allies on the limpid water.

"These (the hues and cries) are foams and bubbles that the U.S. and Israel are trying to create on the clear and limpid water; the U.S. is a wandering and idle bubble; the U.S. is trapped in Iraq quagmire; it neither can remain in Iraq because of hefty economic, social and human cost it has been enduring nor can it leave the country due to its high spendings," said substitute Friday prayers leader of Tehran Ayatollah Mohammad Emami Kashani, refuting Washington's terrorist charges against Iran aimed at preventing the country's membership in the Shanghai Cooperation Organization (SCO).

Addressing large groups of Friday prayers worshipers in Tehran, Ayatollah Kashani said that contrary to the U.S. propaganda, the Chinese Foreign Minister announced Iran is not supporter of terrorism.

He questioned, "How is it that Hizbollah, which is highly popular in Lebanon, is labeled as terrorist? And, how Hamas, that is elected by the Palestinian nation, is terrorist?" Somewhere in his second sermon, Ayatollah Kashani refuted Western and

U.S. propaganda against Iran's peaceful nuclear program and hoped that Tehran's nuclear problem would be settled through diplomacy.

"The government and Supreme National Security Council are hoped to benefit from their active diplomacy and earn lots of blessings for the country through diplomatic ways," announced the Ayatollah.

Boasting success of Iranian youth in mastering peaceful nuclear energy, Ayatollah Kashani said, "We have now achieved the point of knowledge to amaze the westerners. They should know that they can not deprive us of the technology through charges and claims." The cleric denounced conspiracies against Iran, charging it of pursuing nuclear weapons.

"The one, who imposed the eight-year Sacred Defense (the 1980–88 Iran-Iraq war), has made conspiracies today, claiming that the international community has come to the conclusion that Iran is seeking nuclear weapons. Of course, the world will not accept the charge," announced the Ayatollah.

He also condemned a few Western states for the decisions they have been adopting against Iran over its peaceful nuclear program, attempting to justify their decisions echoed international concerns.

"As the Supreme Leader of Islamic Revolution (Ayatollah Seyed Ali Khamenei) has remarked, how can the words and comments, raised by a few people in chambers and announced by certain arrogant mouthpieces, be taken as an international stance?" questioned the major cleric.

He said Iran's peaceful nuclear technology is national and domesticated and "if you ask the world too, they would say Iran is entitled to having such a technology and knowledge." He went on to say that the world and the NAM states, except a few ones and the U.S. and Israel, have been supporting Iran's peaceful nuclear program.[19]

Kashani is also a prominent Shiite cleric who gives the important Friday sermon at Tehran mosques. Here are some of his other statements and sermons. Judge for yourself his intent:

Friday Sermon at Tehran University—Ayatollah Mohammad Emami-Kashani

Channel 1, Iranian TV, July 8, 2005

KASHANI:.... You speak of terror and al Qaeda, have you forgotten who the mother and father of al Qaeda are? America is its father, and Israel its mother. It is the illegitimate child of these powers. You yourselves have brought it about....

CROWD:...Allah Akbar. Khamenei is the leader. Death to those who reject the rule of the jurisprudent. Death to America. Death to England. Death to the hypocrites (Mojahedin-e Khalq) and Saddam. Death to Israel.

KASHANI: You yourselves have brought it about, and you have done so in the name of Islam. Thus, the child, whose father is the arrogance of the White House, and whose mother is the executioners of Israel, and who you have named "Islam"—is known to all. The reason he was named this way is clear, as is your true nature. You brought (al Qaeda) about in order to bring calamity to our lives, but, thank God, it has brought calamity to yours.[20]

Channel 1, Iranian TV, January 28, 2005

**If you Americans behave with disrespect—even just a lit-
tle bit—the Iranian people will punch you in the mouth
so hard that all your devouring teeth will fall out.** (Chanting: "Allah Akbar, Khamenei is the leader, Death to those who
reject the jurisprudent, Death to America, Death to England,
Death to the hypocrites and Saddam, Death to Israel.") One
young Iranian is worth all you Americans. He smiles at your
weapons. Is he afraid? We hope that by the virtue of Muhammad
and his household God will give some brains to the arrogant, to
the enemies, and to the Zionists. Amen.[21]

Channel 1, Iranian TV, October 15, 2004

Mr. America, we are glad that the world today doesn't interpret
the terms democracy, freedom, and fighting terrorism, according
to what you say. We are glad about this. (Chanting: "Death to
America.") We are glad that when the world wants to interpret
these terms it looks at your actions. It looks at what you're doing
and says that this democracy is a lie. Fighting terrorism is a lie.
Supporting the weak and unfortunate in Iraq, Afghanistan, and
other places is a lie. The lie has been exposed and you remain
stubborn. You may remain stubborn but the world is awakening.
The good thing is that you have discarded the mask, revealing your
black face. One should be glad about this.[22]

Channel 1, Iranian TV, August 20, 2004:

Regarding the referendum held a few days ago in Venezuela,
which lead to the failure of America's policy, I wish such a referendum were held in America. The American public would be

asked if it was content with Bush's actions. If the public votes for him, woe betides the American people. Are you, the American public, content with the many crimes your representative commits? Are you content that you pour the blood of the downtrodden into a cup and drink it just like that? Why did your Bush submerge your arms up to the elbows in the blood of the people. What do you want from the Islamic world? As long as you rely on your might, your administration an entire public will say justice is with you. But once you die and are buried, it will not be like that.

History recounts what you perpetrated. There are museums world wide in which the statues of all the rulers stand. Mr. Bush, think about it! After you die people will gaze upon your statue. What does the world say when it gazes upon Nero? What does the world say when it gazes upon Hitler? After all you have committed worse acts then them. Because of these crimes historians will write about you and commentators will comment, and they will send you so many curses and your face will be blackened so much so that only few in the course of history will have faces as black as yours.

You have darkened the face of America in the world. But know this: despite all that you perpetrate, just like your ancestors were beaten in Vietnam until they left, so you will be beaten until you leave Iraq. There are so many proud. Zealous youth in Iran, Pakistan, Lebanon, Saudi Arabia, and the Islamic countries, and they will endanger all your interests. What should Muslims do? Oh Hidden Imam! We are weary. This situation exacts a very high price from us. (crying) By virtue of your father Imam Ali and your mother Fatemeh, ask the Lord to hasten your appearance. Oh God, when will we hear your voice, oh most precious Hidden Imam? [all crying][23]

Channel 1, Iran TV, July 30, 2004:

The West came and separated the heavens from the earth. The West came and separated between life and God. They have become miserable and they don't know what to do. They are unable to take account of their future. They see their existence as hollow.... Hollow and empty. Who empties them? Those same superpowers did it. Those arrogant rich Zionists did this in order to derive pleasure from every boy and girl. I say to the American people: What is this life you are living? Why do you keep silent? What situation are you in? I say to the American people, according to the Koran: "They drive their people into the house of perdition." Your lives are lost, you will collapse. America will collapse. I must tell our youth and the entire Islamic world: The arrogant world is committing all these crimes in order to empty the brains of the youth and send them to drug addiction and a life of decadence and sloth so their brains will be empty and when it (the arrogant world) comes to rob their home, and they will be sleeping, and will not wake up... they will be drunk and will not wake up.[24]

Channel 1, Iran TV, May 7, 2004:

By using power, money, fraud the enemy is interested in gaining control over the world of Islam. Power meaning weapons in unlimited amounts, money fraud, trickery, deception, lies, lies.... So much torture in Iraqi prisons, America says, "never mind, it only appears so." They are not even ashamed to face the people and the world and tell them these things. "It only appears so," Bush says. "It only appears so. The real purpose is that we wish to give Iraq security. We wish to give them democracy." But it seems as though this way you also kill old and young, men and women, humiliating them and being audacious in various ways....The deception is thus: they turn Hamas into a martyr. This deception Sharon and that man Bush standing in America, declaring to the whole world, "We have two types of terror, good terror and bad terror. Good terrorists and Bad terrorist. This is good terror." This is our situation.[25]

"Good terror." That is the business of the ayatollahs.

SIX

The Taliban, Pakistan, and Southwest Asia

East of Iran were the Taliban, defeated by American forces in 2001, but apparently resurgent in the spring of 2007. The Taliban, according to Defense Department sources, have been given sanctuary in and around the Pakistani city of Quetta. Though the U.S. government has given the Pakistanis actionable intelligence that could be used to capture or kill the Taliban leaders, the Pakistanis have so far refused to act. This is almost certainly because the Pakistani Inter-Service Intelligence Agency (ISI) was and is a longtime supporter of the Taliban and the Musharraf government is unable to control the ISI's actions.

The Taliban captured the Afghanistan capital of Kabul in September of 1996. Their nation had been shredded by a decade of war with the Soviet invaders. Afghanistan's history—which goes back at least to the settlement of Herat about 5,000 years ago—was one of almost constant war. The Taliban made an alliance with Osama bin Laden after he had fled Saudi Arabia and enabled him to organize, train, and operate his terrorist organization under their protection.

After September 11, President Bush demanded they surrender bin Laden to us under threat of war, and they refused. American ground and air forces attacked the Taliban in October 2001.

On November 15, 2001, in the midst of the battle to overthrow his regime, Mullah Omar—the still-at-large cleric leader of the Taliban—gave an interview to the BBC. This is the transcript:

What do you think of the current situation in Afghanistan?

You [the BBC] and American puppet radios have created concern. But the current situation in Afghanistan is related to a bigger cause—that is the destruction of America.

And on the other hand, the screening of Taliban [for those who are or are not loyal] is also in process. We will see these things happen within a short while.

What do you mean by the destruction of America? Do you have a concrete plan to implement this?

The plan is going ahead and, God willing, it is being implemented.

But it is a huge task, which is beyond the will and comprehension of human beings.

If God's help is with us, this will happen within a short period of time; keep in mind this prediction.

Osama bin Laden has reportedly threatened that he would use nuclear, chemical, or biological weapons against America. Is your threat related to his?

This is not a matter of weapons. We are hopeful for God's help. The real matter is the extinction of America. And, God willing, it [America] will fall to the ground.

During the past few days, you have lost control of several provinces. Are you hopeful to regain the lost territory?

We are hopeful that you will see the same kind of change that you saw [losing and regaining territory].

What was the reason for the fast retreat? Why have your troops fled the cities? Is it because you suffered heavily from the U.S. bombings or have your soldiers betrayed you?

I told you that it is related to the larger task.

The Taliban may have made some mistakes.

Screening the Taliban [for loyalty] is a big task. And these problems may serve to cleanse [errant Taliban] of their sins. But there is a big change under way on the other side as well.

Can you tell us which provinces are under your control at the moment?

We have four, five provinces. But it is not important how many provinces we have under our control.

Once we did not have a single province, and then the time came when we had all the provinces, which we have lost in a week. So the numbers of the provinces are not important.

As your participation in the future government has already been ruled out—if some of your forces decide to join the future government as representatives of the Taliban in general or to moderate Taliban, will you oppose it?

There is no such thing in the Taliban. All Taliban are moderate. There are two things: extremism ["ifraat," or doing something to excess] and conservatism ["tafreet," or doing something insufficiently]. So in that sense, we are all moderates—taking the middle path.

The struggle for a broad-based government has been going on for the last twenty years, but nothing came of it.

We will not accept a government of wrong-doers. We prefer death than to be a part of an evil government.

I tell you, keep this in mind. This is my prediction. You believe it or not—it's up to you. But we will have to wait and see.[1]

Since then, the Taliban have substantially recovered. Reports in early 2007, confirmed to me by Defense Department sources, are that the Taliban leadership have obtained sanctuary in and around the city of Quetta in southwestern Pakistan. There they have resumed training, arming, and operating their terrorist networks inside Afghanistan. The same Defense Department sources told me that pages and pages of clear, actionable intelligence have been provided to the Pakistanis, but they have refused to act against the Taliban or to allow American forces to strike against them on Pakistani territory.

Nevertheless, at this writing—April 2007—American forces in southern and eastern Afghanistan are attacking and destroying sub-

stantial Taliban forces there. This proves the need to continue our attention to what the Taliban are saying, as well as the Pakistanis.

Pakistani president Pervez Musharraf should be credited with enormous cooperation with us in the war against the Taliban. But Musharraf has an internal problem: the ISI, which is a government-within-a-government and not under his control. Musharraf runs hot and cold, dodging rhetorical bullets so he does not have to dodge real ones from ISI.

Musharraf's problem is very direct and simple: the ISI created the Taliban regime and remains more loyal to it than to Musharraf.

In a 2006 interview, according to a report in the Telegraph of London, "retired Pakistani intelligence officers could be running the Taliban insurgency against coalition forces in Afghanistan, Pakistan's president, Gen. Pervez Musharraf, has said. He made the admission to an American television channel at the weekend—the first time he had broken from his usual policy of denying any Pakistani hand in the rebellion against coalition forces in Afghanistan. 'I have some reports that some dissidents, some people, retired people who were in the forefront in ISI during the period of 1979 to 89, may be assisting with their links somewhere here and there. We are keeping a very tight watch and we'll get a hold of them if that happens.'"

The Telegraph report contined, saying, "Gen. Musharraf's remarks confirmed suspicions long held by western diplomats. Gen. Musharraf has hitherto fiercely rejected the claims, saying during a visit to Britain last week that the West would be 'brought to its knees' without Pakistan's help. 'Remember my words: if the ISI is not with you and Pakistan is not with you, you will lose in Afghanistan,' he said."[2]

Musharraf bears watching, and deserves both support and pressure to assert American interests in his nation and its neighbors:

Afghanistan and India. Pakistan is armed with nuclear weapons and the means to deliver them with ballistic missiles. Its now-retired (we hope) chief nuclear scientist, A.Q. Khan, was the principal proliferator of nuclear weapons technology and, with the Russians, put Iran on its path to achieving nuclear weapons in the next few years. If Musharraf is removed, the next Pakistani ruler may be more inclined to revive the Khan network, openly supplying nuclear weapons and technology to Iran and other terrorist states.

Fighting the Ideological War[3]

We aren't fighting a war against terrorists to win the hearts and minds of the Middle East. We are fighting it to end the threat of terrorism. Victory can't be achieved with bullets and bombs alone. This is, at its core, an ideological war. Just as we defeated communism by defeating the communists' ideology, we need to attack and destroy that of the radical Islamists.

To do that, we first have to understand that radical Islam—the Islam of Mahmoud Ahmadinejad, Osama bin Laden, and the rest— isn't a religion. It is an ideology that cobbles totalitarianism together with a messianic vision of religious nationalism. Radical Islam (unlike the actual religion) tolerates no other religion, and demands that its adherents give up the basic human freedoms enshrined in our Bill of Rights. No freedom of speech, no free press, no fair trials by a jury of your peers, only enslavement. Like the Nazis, the radical Islamists play on the sense of persecution and cultural inferiority that many people in underdeveloped nations possess because they are oppressed. And, like the Nazis, the Islamists have convinced their followers that the problems of their world are the fault of others. The Islamists blame every ill of their world on America, the West, the Jews, and Israel. Like the Soviets, the Islamists believe that their enslavement of the world is inevitable (though, unlike the Soviets, they believe it is God's will that they must succeed). Its adherents, like the Nazis and the Communists before them, believe their victory is both inevitable and irreversible. That is a powerful ideology which we have yet to engage with the necessary weapons.

We fought the Soviet ideology from 1946 to 1989. In those years, we rode our own ideological roller coaster. For many Americans— and many more Europeans, Africans, and others around the world—the only weapon in that ideological battle was self-criticism. They were willing to confuse healthy criticism of our own system of government with praise for the Soviet counterparts. They were even willing to deny the horrific repressions, mass murder, and subjugation by force of other peoples.

The Soviet ideology was defeated, and the Cold War won, by the Soviets' self-imposed poverty, our military buildup, and by the fact that we proved to the world—by objective comparison—that their enslavement of people was inferior to our freedoms. It was neither fashionable nor even polite conversation to say, as Ronald Reagan and Margaret Thatcher did relentlessly, that our system of freedom was objectively superior to Soviet oppression. That constant ideological pounding, coupled with the physical courage and intellectual mastery of Aleksandr Solzhenitsyn and Lech Walesa, won the ideological battle of the Cold War. We have to do the same in this war, and in much the same way.

Our military—comprised of many of the best people our country has ever produced—is winning every fight it enters. But it can't win the war alone. Our politicians have to do that by fighting the ideological war. The Chairman of the Joint Chiefs, General Peter Pace,

understands this better than any of our pols. In his "guidance" to the
Joint Staff, published right after he took the job, Pace said that, "Our
enemies are violent extremists who would deny us, and all mankind,
the freedom to choose our own destiny. Finding this distributed,
loosely networked enemy is the greatest challenge we face. We must
find and defeat them in an environment where information, percep-
tion, and how and what we communicate are every bit as critical as
the application of traditional kinetic effects." So how do we do it?

President Bush needs to lead us in the ideological fight, just as
Ronald Reagan did in the Cold War. We need to hear from him—
and the rest of our leaders—the kind of blunt comparisons we heard
from Reagan. Radical Islam enslaves people. It robs them of the
inalienable rights endowed by their creator that our Declaration of
Independence described, and our Constitution protects. Our society
is as prosperous as any in the world, and that is a direct result of the
freedoms we enjoy. Radical Islam condemns its adherents and its
slaves to poverty and suffering. And the nations that support it are
our enemies.

We have the ability to tell right from wrong and good from evil
and there is no need for us to apologize for that. Nor should we twist
our relations with other countries to suit some false moral equiva-
lence. Those who say, for example, that if India or Israel can have
nuclear weapons why shouldn't Iran, are guilty of illogic. It is permissible for us, and the rest of the free world, to say that some countries are evil and others are not, and to condition our relations with
them all on the basis of our own judgment. To deliver that judgment,
and act upon it, is the job of the president.

In time of war, the president of the United States has to be the
boldest spokesman for freedom in the world. President Bush needs
to be fighting this ideological battle with all the energy and relent-

lessness of a marine sergeant assaulting a bunch of terrorists holed up in a cave. In the Cold War, Ronald Reagan stood fast and spoke clearly without fear of offending the enemy, because he knew that a war between ideologies cannot be fought with soft words and euphemisms. What was true for the Cold War is no less true today. It's not enough to say that we fight tyranny. It is essential to say that we fight for what is right, and what is by any measure better than the enemy will ever deliver to even its most loyal followers.

SEVEN

Radical Islam Aims at Turkey

Turkey, since the achievement of Attaturk, has been the most modernized Islamic nation. A cornerstone of NATO for decades, it was neglected and rejected in the Clinton era. Its prime minister, Turgut Ozal, died in 1993. Ozal had been a strong leader, making Turkey more free and open to cultural evolution than any other Islamic nation. When he died, neither President Clinton nor Vice President Gore took the trouble to attend the funeral. It was an insult Turks will remember for decades to come.

Since Ozal's death, Turkey has been dragged away from Western influence by the same ideological surge that has affected Arab nations. It is now on the verge of becoming an Islamist state. The battle of ideas goes on in Turkey. Are the Islamists winning? Judge for yourself.

Dünya (Turkey), February 9, 2005:

"The Biggest Danger: USA"

In the Turkish business daily Dunya, columnist Dr. Burhan Ozfatura, who is a former mayor of Izmir, wrote:

It is my sincere belief that the USA is the biggest danger for Turkey, today and in the future. At the present the USA is run by an incompetent, very aggressive, true enemy of Islam, brainwashed with evangelical nonsense, a bloodthirsty team that is a loyal link in Israel's command and control chain.

- Afghanistan is destroyed for U.S. interests.
- Iraq has become a bloodbath. People are nostalgic for the days of the cruel Saddam.
- As a result, sooner or later, it will be Turkey's turn. Because their [Israel's] "Promised Land" includes a large chunk of Turkish territory. Israel aspires to be the sole power in the area. Therefore, it cannot tolerate a strong Turkey in any leadership role.

Unfortunately, we as the Turkish nation have a weak memory. Otherwise we would never have forgotten:

- All the USA's plots and the support they gave to the Armenians, during our Independence War
- How they betrayed us during the Korean War
- All the concessions they gave to the Russians after World War II
- How Kennedy sold Turkey during the Cuban crisis
- Johnson's disrespectful letter
- That it is the USA that planned and financed the PKK affair, the "large Armenia scenario," Greek aggression and demands (Greek ecumenical ambitions, Greek Orthodox support,

Byzantium dreams and aspirations), today's widespread missionary activities, Alavi-Kurd incitements

- The evil work done in our country by the "peace volunteers"
- The U.S. threats after our parliament refused to take part in the massacres in Iraq, the incident of tying and putting sacks on the heads of our soldiers and their capture in Iraq, organizing the massacre of the Turkmen, supporting the likes of Talabani and Barzani—all in order to serve their own interests
- The U.S. activities in northern Iraq for the establishment of "an independent Kurdish state"
- The U.S.'s adherence to the worthless Sevres Treaty, its masterminding of the [Armenian] genocide-allegations, (and the fact that America still has not signed on to the LaUSAnne Agreement)
- That they [the U.S.] are behind all the coups [in Turkey]
- That the pre–September 12 [September 12 refers to the 1980 military coup in Turkey that followed political unrest and Left-Right clashes on campuses. In 1983, power was transferred back to a civilian government] events all originated in American universities

Sadly, at present Turkey is under total invasion by the USA:

- The Turkish economy is under complete control of the U.S. through the IMF and the World Bank (even our demographic and genetic codes are in their hands)
- Our military is dependent on the U.S. (how soon we forgot all the bad things and the embargo they imposed on us, after our operation in Cyprus)
- There is a cultural invasion [of Turkey] by the U.S.

- We have no secrets and can hide nothing from America. Even our "intelligence" is guided by the CIA.
- Our natural resources (including oil) are controlled by America. (Not even one-thousandth of our reserves is mined. All our riches like gold, borax, thorium, uranium, must urgently be utilized in cooperation with other friendly countries.)
- Our agricultural sector (through the IMF) is directly guided by the USA (e.g., No measures can ever be taken against Cargill, even if our national interests dictate it.)

In short, we are dependent on the U.S., to every last detail. And unfortunately, it is not possible to overcome all [of the above], with our present foreign policy of "status quo."

Both the ruling party and the opposition lack courage. They all believe in the necessity of getting along with the U.S. They fear provocations and choose to believe the great lie of "strategic alliance" [with America].

We consider it a national duty to alert the nation to these dangers. We hope for the enactment of a totally independent "National Defense Policy." We want cooperation with forces that are independent of American influence. We remind you that the mentally unbalanced Bush and his team (servants of corporate special interests) should not be trusted. (I strongly believe that the U.S. had its hand in the earthquakes of Istanbul-Izmit and the recent Southeast Asia disasters.)[1]

Milli Gazete (Turkey), February 5, 2005

"America's Hitler"

In the pan-Islamist daily Milli Gazete, *columnist Süleyman Arif Emre wrote:*

As we know, Germany's Hitler started World War II, and about 50 million people perished because of Hitler's ambitions. Bush is America's Hitler. Like Hitler, he too has become a curse for the world. If the world's sensible leaders don't unite against Bush to stop him, a great number of people will die because of his ambitions. Hitler was very racist. Bush, who is an ally of the Zionists, belongs to the racist philosophy too. The beliefs of Bush's evangelical church coupled with Jewish racism, which exceeds Hitler's, are sufficient proof that the "Sharon and Bush duo" are militants of the same fanatical philosophy. Hitler said that he would establish a new world order if Germany won. Bush is after similar invasions. First he targeted Afghanistan and Iraq. Later he expanded his invasion map to include twenty-two more Islamic countries where he wants to change the order and the borders. He says that he wants to bring the likes of Karzai and Allawi [to these countries] to power, and in doing so establish his colonial empire. When a person goes rabid, there is no stopping him. God forbid, if he succeeds in occupying those twenty-two countries, his lust will expand to cover the whole world. Why expand? Because the five-thoUSAnd-year-old dream of the Zionists is to grasp the valleys of both the Nile and Euphrates and build a Jewish state to rule the rest of the world. What I want to say is that the end game for the "Sharon and Bush duo" is to build a state that would rule the world, just like it was for Hitler.

What I am saying is beyond a mere guess. Bush yesterday laid out the next steps of his invasion plans and blurted out the names of Iran, Syria, Saudi Arabia and Egypt....

Conclusion: It is clear that these developments will finally come to the end that our beloved Prophet [Mohammed] promised us. Our Prophet Lord said: Around the time of "judgment day" there will be a war between my peoples [Muslim believers] and the Jews. And the Jews will be vanquished. During that war the rocks will speak and say, "O Muslim, there is a zionist hiding behind me, come and kill him."[2]

Tercüman (Turkey), January 20, 2005

Turks are "The Gold Medalists in Anti-Americanism"

In the mainstream moderate-right daily Tercuman, columnist Cengiz Çandar wrote:

The BBC surveyed about 22,000 people all around the world between November 15, 2004 and January 5, 2005. Forty-seven percent of the respondents expressed the opinion that "America's influence on the world is very negative."

What is especially interesting is that among those with the most negative view on America's policies under Bush are the Turks, heading the list with 82 percent. The Turks are followed by the Argentineans with 79 percent, and the Brazilians with 78 percent.

This means that we are the gold medalists in "anti-Americanism." [According to the survey]...among the Muslim countries, Turkey is followed [in anti-Bush sentiment] by Indonesia and Lebanon.[3]

EIGHT

China: The Emerging Enemy

Observe calmly, secure our position, cope with affairs calmly, hide our capacities and bide our time; be good at maintaining a low profile; and never claim leadership.

— DENG XIAOPING, former paramount leader of the People's Republic of China, *The Twenty-Four Characters Strategy*, c. 1990.

While America is at war with the Islamofascists, other adversaries act. It is arguable which is most dangerous, but we cannot afford to limit the attention we pay to any of them.

China is an emerging superpower. In history—from Rome's conquest of empire to the United States rising from the ashes of Europe after World War II—no nation has ever risen to superpower rank except on a tide of war. China's military spending—most of it secret, concealed not only from us but from the Chinese people—appears to be at a pace unseen since Germany of the 1930s.

China is ruled by a dictator, Hu Jintao, whose regime has been labeled as among the worst dictatorships in the world:

Despite China's economic liberalization, President Hu Jintao's government remains one of the most repressive. Some 250,000 Chinese are serving sentences in "re-education" and labor camps. China executes more people than all other nations combined, often for nonviolent crimes. The death penalty can be given for burglary, embezzlement, counterfeiting, bribery, or killing a panda. Hu's government controls all media and Internet use. Defense lawyers who argue too vigorously for clients' rights may be disbarred or imprisoned. And if minorities (such as Tibetans) speak out for autonomy, they're labeled "terrorists," imprisoned, and tortured.[1]

Hu, we must note, was China's ruler of Tibet at the time of the June 1989 Tiananmen Square massacre. He was one of the first CCP (Chinese Communist Party) leaders to express support for the massacre.

Because China is a totalitarian state, and controls the media and the Internet as totally as any other, we get few glimpses into the thinking of its top leaders and even fewer into that of their subordinates. That is why the 1999 book Unrestricted Warfare *is either tremendously important or deserving of being tossed in a pile of military fiction.[2] It is an exaggeration to say that the book is a plan to make war on America. But it is also an understatement to characterize it as only an exercise in academic military theory. It is, in fact, a blueprint to modernize China's military forces and strategies in order to defeat the United States.*

Many Western analysts are quick to deride it because it is written by two PLA colonels—Qiao Liang and Wang Xiangsui—who are certainly too low-ranking to be able to set official policy. Before we consider some of their statements, it is essential to read one of the authors' acknowledgments at the end of the book:

Upon the occasion of the publication of this book, we would like to here sincerely thank the Chief-of-Staff Cheng Butao and Assistant Chief-of-Staff Huang Guorong, of the PLA Literature and Arts Publishing House for their unswerving support whereupon this book was able to be so quickly published within such a short period of time.[3]

In a nation in which the government and military are one and the same, Unrestricted Warfare could not—short of a written introduction by Hu Jintao—have a more official endorsement.

The principal point of Unrestricted Warfare is that the modern battlefield is not just on the ground where massed armies may square off against each other. The battlefield, say Liang and Xiangsui, is everywhere. Financial markets, civilian populations, the media, all are the proper objects—and tools—of war. They mock American reliance on technological warfare.

In a section they title, "The Illness of Extravagance, and Zero Casualties," the authors write, like bin Laden does, of the vulnerability of American opinion to the costs of war. They, like the Islamofascists, believe all that is necessary to defeat America is to cause enough deaths among American troops that the nation will lose the will to win:

If you cannot make out the overtones of my praises and only think they are proud of the American military for having fully realized their war objectives by defeating Iraq [in the 1991 Gulf War] with the aid of high-technology weapons, then you may think that this however is the typical nonsense spoken by two who have different opinions regarding the ability of technology to bring success, and you also are not yet fully aware of the meaning

of American-style warfare. What you must know is that this is a
nationality that has never been willing to pay the price of life,
and, moreover, has always vied for victory at all costs. The
appearance of high-technology weaponry can now satisfy these
extravagant hopes of the American people. During the Gulf War,
of 500,000 troops there were only 148 fatalities and 458 wounded.
Goals that they long since only dreamt of were finally realized—
"no casualties."

Ever since the Vietnam War, both the military and American
society have been sensitized to human casualties during military
operations, almost to the point of morbidity. Reducing casualties
and achieving war objectives have become two equal weights on
the American military scale. These common American soldiers
who should be on the battlefield have now become the most
costly security in war, like precious china bowls that people are
afraid to break. All of the opponents who have engaged in battle
with the American military have probably mastered the secret of
success—if you have no way of defeating this force, you should
kill its rank and file soldiers.

This point, taken from the U.S. Congressional Report's
emphasis on "reducing casualties is the highest objective in for-
mulating the plan," can be unequivocally confirmed. "Pursuit of
zero casualties," this completely compassionate simple slogan, has
actually become the principal motivating factor in creating American-style extravagant warfare.[4]

*Liang and Xiangsui write that because the battlefield is everywhere,
and every tool a weapon, any successful war against a nation such
as America must be carried out by non-traditional means in military
operations other than conventional war:*

The weapons used...can be airplanes, cannons, poison gas bombs, bio-chemical agents, as well as computer viruses, net browsers, and financial derivative tools.[5]

A modern attack, they postulate, would be one in which conventional military forces are almost irrelevant:

...if the attacking side secretly musters large amounts of capital without the enemy nation being aware of this at all and launches a sneak attack against financial markets, then after causing a financial crisis, buries a computer virus and hacker detachment in the opponent's computer system in advance, while at the same time carrying out a network attack against the enemy so that civilian electricity network, traffic dispatching network, financial transaction network, telephone communications network and mass media network are completely paralyzed, this will cause the enemy nation to fall into social panic, street riots, and a political crisis. There is finally the forceful bearing down by the army, and military means are utilized in gradual stages until the enemy is forced to sign a dishonorable peace treaty.[6]

Is this just a flight of fancy by military theorists? Seven years after Unrestricted Warfare *was published in China, the Pentagon's report to Congress said:*

China's computer network operations (CNO) include computer network attack, computer network defense, and computer network exploitation. The PLA sees CNO as critical to seize the initiative and achieve "electromagnetic dominance" early in a conflict, and as a force multiplier. Although there is no evidence of a formal Chinese CNO doctrine, PLA theorists have coined the term "Integrated Network Electronic Warfare" to outline the integrated use of electronic warfare, CNO, and limited kinetic strikes against key [command, control, communications, and computer] nodes to disrupt the enemy's battlefield communications. The PLA has established information warfare units to develop viruses to attack enemy computer systems and networks, and tactics and measures to protect friendly computer systems and networks. The PLA has increased the role of CNO in its military exercises. For example, exercises in 2005 began to incorporate offensive operations, primarily in first strikes against enemy networks.[7]

In that context, we can examine the statements of China's leadership.

Hu Jintao's People's Republic of China has allied itself to every nation our State Department lists as a state sponsor of terrorism. Each of those nations lists China as a trading partner, and with trade comes the influence of the People's Liberation Army (which includes China's navy, air force, and missile forces). To fully explain China is not my purpose here. It is only to call attention to what the Chinese leadership says.

China views Taiwan as a renegade province, not a nation entitled to freedom. The PRC makes no secret of its plan to take Taiwan peacefully or otherwise. And it brooks no hint of interference by the United States.

In 2005, a professor at China's National Defense University, Gen. Zhu Chenghu threatened nuclear war over Taiwan. He said:

If the Americans are determined to interfere [then] we will be determined to respond....We...will prepare ourselves for the destruction of all of the cities east of Xian. **Of course, the Americans will have to be prepared that hundreds . . . of cities will be destroyed by the Chinese.**[8]

Heritage Foundation visiting fellow Larry Wortzel, who attended Zhu's speech, reportedly offered the general a way out, asking if he meant only that China would respond with nuclear weapons if America first attacked China with them. According to one report, Zhu insisted that a nuclear response would occur even if America interfered with conquest of Taiwan using conventional weapons.[9] When a public uproar ensued, China disavowed Zhu's remarks.[10] The disavowal is entirely consistent with China's "Twenty-four Character Strategy."

China regards its neighbors in much the same way as Japan's imperial government regarded theirs in the 1930s. Instead of calling them a "Greater East Asia co-prosperity sphere" as the Japanese did, China calls them "peripheral nations." The purpose of China's military growth is to assert hegemony over them.

In a January 2005 interview, Lieutenant General Liu Yazhou, currently Deputy Political Commissar of the PLA Air Force, discussed this dynamic in a more abstract form:

. . . when a nation grows strong enough, it practices hegemony. The sole purpose of power is to pursue even greater power. . . . Geography is destiny . . . when a country begins to rise, it should first set itself in an invincible position.[11]

In 2002, Hu Jintao was only China's vice president. Even then, he warned against American interference in China's "reunification" with Taiwan, warning against the sale of weapons to Taiwan with which it could defend against China's "reunification" plans:

The question of Taiwan has always been the most important and most sensitive issue at the heart of China-U.S. relations. Properly handling this question is the key to promoting our constructive and cooperative relations. If any trouble occurs on the Taiwan question, it would be difficult for China-U.S. relations to move forward, and a retrogression may even occur. The question of Taiwan is China's internal matter and should be resolved by the Chinese people on both sides of the Taiwan Straits. Since Nixon took office as president, the successive U.S. administrations, both Republican and Democratic, have been committed to the One-China policy and the Three Joint Communiqués. That serves the interests of both China and the U.S., and is an act of wisdom and political vision. Selling sophisticated weapons to Taiwan or upgrading U.S.-Taiwan relations is inconsistent with the foregoing commitments, serving neither peace and stability in the Taiwan Straits nor China-U.S. relationship and the common interests of the two countries. It is our hope that the U.S. side will strictly honor its commitments to the Chinese side and play a constructive role in China's peaceful reunification.[12]

That view apparently applies more broadly than to Taiwan. In 2005, a top Chinese official warned against American alliances on its periphery, even with Australia:

Chinese Foreign Ministry's top Pacific policy official, Mr. He Yafei, told an interviewer from *The Australian,* "If there were any move by Australia and the U.S. in terms of that alliance [ANZUS] that is detrimental to peace and stability in Asia, then it [Australia] has to be very careful," adding that this was "especially so" in the case of Taiwan.[13]

The breadth of the view—that China's military power must be extended over its neighbors—is repeated often. For example, according to the Pentagon's 2006 report, "Gen. Wen Zongren, then political commissar of the elite PLA Academy of Military Science, stated in March 2005 that resolving the Taiwan issue is of 'far-reaching significance to breaking international forces' blockage against China's maritime security. . . . Only when we break this blockade shall we be able to talk about China's rise.'"[14]

On August 13, 2001 the New York Times interviewed then president Jiang Zemin. The following is a summary of this interview by the Chinese embassy in Canada.

On the anti-missile issue, Jiang said that China's position on the anti-missile issue can be summarized in two main points. Firstly, we are not in favor of the said move. We share the worries of many other countries that this move may cause a series of negative effects and thus impair world strategic stability. Secondly, we stand for working out, through dialogue, solutions that would not harm security interests of any side. China's possession of the very limited nuclear weapons is solely for self-defense and poses no threat to any country. In order to safeguard our national security interests, we need to ensure the effectiveness of our nuclear force.

On the Taiwan question, Jiang said: Taiwan is part of Chinese territory. The Taiwan question bears on the national pride of the entire Chinese people, the sovereignty, territorial integrity, and development of China. All the Chinese people are looking forward to an early settlement of the question. This is the very aspiration of the people. Any attempt to split Taiwan from China will never get anywhere. China is bound to achieve complete reunification.

People living on both sides of the Taiwan Straits are Chinese. Blood is thicker than water. No one else is more eager than us for a peaceful solution to the Taiwan question. It is precisely for the purpose of safeguarding the interests of our Taiwan compatriots to the fullest extent that we have proposed and stuck to the basic principle of "peaceful reunification and one country, two systems." However, we cannot renounce the use of force. If we did, a peaceful reunification would become impossible. There are three joint communiqués between China and the U.S., i.e., the 1972 Shanghai Joint Communiqué, the 1979 Joint Communiqué on the Establishment of Diplomatic Relations and the Joint Communiqué issued on August 17th, 1982. They together constitute the political foundation of the China-U.S. relationship. In the three joint communiqués, the U.S. clearly commits itself to the one-China policy. In the August 17 Communiqué, it states that it does not seek to carry out a long-term policy of arms sales to Taiwan and that it intends gradually to reduce its sale of arms to Taiwan, leading, over a period of time, to a final resolution. The treaty, however, is that over all these years, the U.S. has never stopped selling sophisticated arms to China's Taiwan. Furthermore, it has upgraded its arms sales to Taiwan in both quantitative and qualitative terms. This has deeply hurt the Chinese people, interfered in China's internal affairs, and made a peaceful solution to the Taiwan question more difficult. Such practice of the U.S. will not only affect the stability in the Taiwan Straits and hinder the improvement of China-U.S. relations, but also harm its own interest in the end.[15]

China (and Russia, as we shall see in the next chapter) share an aversion to American missile defense systems or anything else that might protect American citizens from an attack. Disarmament and new treaties to limit American defense options are always in their minds.

The following are excerpts of a statement by Mr. Liu Jieyi, Director-General of Arms Control and Disarmament Department, Ministry of Foreign Affairs of China, at the Fourth China-U.S. Conference on Arms Control, Disarmament and Non-Proliferation on March 4, 2002, in Washington, D.C.:

. . . . The theme of this conference is "Building a Global Strategic Framework for the Twenty-first Century," a theme of great significance today. At the beginning of the new century, the global security environment is undergoing profound changes. We are faced with a new situation where both traditional and non-traditional security factors are at work and non-traditional security threats are on the rise. At the same time, the decision to withdraw from the ABM Treaty brings a new challenge to global strategic stability and balance as well as the international arms control and disarmament system. Against such a backdrop, all governments need to consider what kind of a new global strategic framework should be built, so as to safeguard effectively world peace and stability in the twenty-first century.

On this issue, I would like to present the following views: First, the fundamental objective of a new global strategic framework should be the common security for all countries. The process of globalization has further deepened the interdependence between countries. This is true both economically and in terms of security. Never before has security been so mutual and indivisible. The security of one country cannot be achieved at the expense of that of others, still less be based on the insecurity of others. Absolute security of oneself does not exist. A new global strategic framework can be stable and long-lasting only if it enhances universal security.

Secondly, a new global strategic framework should be based on the integrity of and universal adherence to the norms of international law. The most prominent feature of the global security situation in the twenty-first century is its uncertainty and the instability that may ensue. To reduce uncertainty and enhance stability, it is critical to establish and maintain a rule-based international security structure. The UN Charter and other universally recognized norms governing international relations should be strictly abided by. As for arms control, disarmament and non-proliferation, a comprehensive legal system has been established so far, thanks to the joint efforts by the international community over decades. This system has become part and parcel of the global collective security architecture centered around the United Nations. It has played an important role in maintaining world peace and security, and has provided necessary predictability in the evolution of the global security landscape. Any weakening of this legal system will inevitably impact negatively on global security and stability.

Thirdly, international cooperation is the only effective way to build a stable global strategic framework. With the world getting smaller, the threats to global security are becoming increasingly diversified and globalized. Non-traditional threats, such as terrorism and transnational crimes, are taking the place of geo-political inter-state confrontation as the biggest challenge to world peace and security. Under such circumstances, multilateral cooperation is not a matter of choice, but a matter of course. Lasting peace and security can only be achieved through international cooperation and in a comprehensive manner rather than by the simple use of force. There is an emerging consensus among the international community that security should be sought through cooperation, dialogue and mutual trust. Without international cooperation, a stable global strategic framework would remain elusive.

Fourthly, a stable global strategic framework should contain the following basic elements:

A) Continued nuclear disarmament and a diminished role for nuclear weapons. To transcend the Cold War mindset, it is first and foremost necessary to jettison the nuclear deterrence policy based on the first use of nuclear weapons. This will go a long way to diminishing the role of nuclear weapons, and greatly contribute to nuclear nonproliferation. The nuclear arms reductions under discussion between major nuclear powers should be irreversible and verifiable. This will help enhance the predictability of global security situation, maintain world peace and stability, and promote international nuclear disarmament process.

B) Non-deployment or development of missile defense systems that undermine the global strategic stability and balance. Confronted with the rising non-traditional security threats, all countries have to reconsider their security strategy and security priorities. The terrorist attacks on September 11 have testified that a missile defense system is not the way to counter terrorist attacks and new security challenges in the twenty-first century. Such a system will not facilitate mutual trust or cooperation among countries or contribute to any country's security.

C) Non-proliferation of weapons of mass destruction (WMD). The non-traditional security threats, as demonstrated by the terrorist attack on September 11 and the anthrax incident have highlighted the importance and urgency of preventing the proliferation of WMD. The proliferation of WMD has complicated causes and backgrounds. To resolve the problem, we should enhance international cooperation and build up an international non-proliferation system participated by all countries. A simplified approach, such as pressure, sanctions or even the threat or use of force, will not resolve the problem, and can only undermine the foundation of cooperation.

D) No arms race in outer space. With the rapid development of science and technology, peaceful development and utilization of outer space for the benefit of mankind has become a reality. The weaponization of outer space will lead to severe consequences and is extremely harmful to the global strategic stability. In the new century, we should prevent outer space from becoming another arena of arms race.

China and the United States are both Permanent Members of the UN Security Council and Nuclear-Weapon-States. The two countries share common interests on many major international issues and both undertake important responsibilities. It is fair to say that it is impossible and even unimaginable to build a new stable global strategic framework without the participation of and cooperation between China and the U.S. On our part, we are ready to join hands with the U. S. in an effort to create a peaceful, stable, dynamic and prosperous new century. The prospects for Sino-U.S. cooperation are broad and bright.

Naturally, China and the U.S. also have differences on issues such as global strategic framework, arms control, disarmament, and non-proliferation. Yet, these differences are by no means unbridgeable. They can be resolved or managed through dialogue and cooperation. At present, there are two issues between China and the U.S. in the field of arms control and nonproliferation that have drawn extensive attention. First is the issue of missile defense. On this issue, I would like to stress that China's disapproval of the U.S. missile defense program is out of concerns about the global strategic stability and the international arms control and disarmament process. China does not threaten any country, and has no intention to conduct nuclear or conventional arms race with any country. On the contrary, China is an important force for peace. It will continue to adhere to its long-standing policy of no-first-use of nuclear weapons and no-use of nuclear weapons against non-nuclear-weapon states and nuclear-weapon-free-zones. China will continue to exercise restraint in the development of nuclear weapons.

The U.S. side has stated on many occasions that its missile defense program is not targeted at China. We expect this to be translated into concrete actions. Meanwhile, Taiwan should not be incorporated into such a missile defense system, nor be provided with missile defense technology. We also hope that the U.S. takes a prudent attitude towards its missile defense cooperation with Japan, so as to avoid jeopardizing regional peace and stability. We are ready to continue to have serious and honest dialogue with the U.S. on the issue of missile defense.

Second is the issue of non-proliferation. China and the U.S. share important common interests and overall objectives on non-proliferation. Both countries are opposed to the proliferation of WMD and advocate that concrete measures should be taken to address the threats posed by such proliferation. In recent years, China has actively supported international efforts to build and strengthen multilateral non-proliferation regimes with universal participation. China has also further enhanced and improved its export control of relevant items and technologies. We are willing to further conduct consultations and cooperation with the U.S. on the issue of non-proliferation and seek appropriate solutions.

The course that the Sino-U.S. relationship has traversed has not always been smooth. But this relationship has been moving forward despite all the twists and turns. It is gratifying that President Bush has just concluded a successful visit to China, and that the relevant authorities of the two countries have also carried out useful consultations. All these developments have given a new impetus to the further development of our bilateral relationship and the establishment of a new global strategic framework. We believe that a mature and stable Sino-U.S. relationship is not only in the interests of both countries, but also has an important bearing on world peace, security, and stability. . . .

Remember President Reagan saying, "trust, but verify"? Add to that a reflex action. When an adversary of the United States speaks of "stability," check your wallet. Your pocket is being picked.

China is also using its client state, North Korea, to assert pressure against American interests and American allies such as Japan which are among China's "peripheral nations." When North Korea tests missiles or develops nuclear weapons, guess whose fault it is?

China's Foreign Ministry spokesperson Kong Quan gave a press conference in September 2003. Below are excerpts of the conference:[16]

Q: You said that you are not disappointed by the statement made by the DPRK [Democratic People's Republic of Korea/North Korea] after the talks. But later the DPRK also said that it had no choice but to enhance its nuclear capability. Under such circumstance, can you tell us whether the next round of talks will be held in Beijing and when we can know the specific time?

A: In the six-party talks, various parties all made clear their positions. Frankly speaking there are both many important consensus and serious differences, especially between the DPRK and the U.S. The tension between the two sides has lasted for over fifty years, with policy factor in between including the U.S. policy towards the DPRK. After the talks, all parties need some time to study seriously the positions of the others and consider the principles of the next phase. We hope that all parties can, proceeding from safeguarding peace and stability in Asia and the world, continue to make efforts towards the direction of solving the question peacefully through dialogue and diplomacy. I can not answer precisely when the next round of talks will be held. It needs to be discussed by the parties. As to whether the next round of talks will be held in Beijing, the Chinese side is flexible and open on this. So long as the proposals are conducive to the peaceful settlement of the question, we will give them positive consideration since our ultimate goal is to solve the question peacefully, ensure denuclearization on the peninsula, and safeguard peace and stability on the peninsula, Asia and the world at large.

Q: Vice Foreign Minister Wang Yi strongly hinted in Manila that the U.S. policy towards the DPRK was the main obstacle to the peaceful settlement of the question. Can you further explain which U.S. policies need to be changed?

A: The antagonism and disputes between the DPRK and the U.S. are serious. The DPRK said that it was under threat and the negative U.S. policy created serious obstacles to it. This all shows the lack of mutual trust between them. We therefore hope that the two sides can further expound their concerns and considerations through further talks, make clear their hopes and demands, keep contact and communication and narrow difference through talks so as to lay a foundation for the peaceful settlement of the question. As to the detailed questions like how the U.S. threatens the DPRK, these are all questions that need to be further discussed in the next round of talks and especially between the U.S. and the DPRK.

When President Bush announced publicly that we were considering opting out of the so-called Anti-Ballistic Missile Treaty that banned defenses against missile attack, China was speaking out against it, saying it would "destabilize" relations. The Beijing regime doesn't want to go the way of the Soviets.

04/10/2001: At the 2001 Disarmament Commission held at the UN headquarters in New York, Chinese ambassador for disarmament Hu Xiaodi said:

■ The U.S. promotion of the NMD system is a unilateral nuclear arms expansion in disguised form, which will seriously impede the progress of international arms control and disarmament, and will possibly trigger a new round of arms race.... A relative stability in balance of power among major countries in the world, and the global strategic stability based on this balance of power, is the premise and condition for attainment of progress in the arms control process related to international disarmament. A relevant country owns the world's most advanced nuclear arsenal and the most sophisticated conventional weapons at the present time, and abides by a nuclear deterrence policy with the core of being the first to use nuclear weapons. Under this condition, the NMD system will definitely become a multiplier of offensive weapons for this country, which will not only seriously hinder the development of the nuclear disarmament process advocated by the United States, Russia and the whole world, but will also render any proposals on reduction of offensive nuclear weapons meaningless.

■ The U.S. promotion of the NMD system will seriously damage the global strategic balance and stability, and harm the mutual trust and cooperation among major powers.... In order to develop and deploy the NMD system, the United States must surmount the Anti-missile Treaty first. Indeed, the Anti-missile Treaty is a product of the Cold War. However, like all other arms control treaties, what the Anti-missile Treaty reflects is a relationship of interdependence between the two signing parties in terms of security. This relationship did not disappear due to the end of the Cold War; instead, the relationship has been further strengthened due to the arrival of globalization.

■ The U.S. promotion of the NMD system will also seriously damage the anti-proliferation mechanism and related efforts. Weapons of mass destruction and proliferation of missiles is a complicated global issue. The establishment of the NMD system is not favorable for the resolution of this issue; instead, it will stimulate further proliferation of missiles, which will in turn upset the foundation of the international anti-proliferation mechanism.

■ The U.S. practice is unfavorable for safeguarding the international peace and security. No matter whether the United States can truly posses the missile defense capability, the U.S. practice will further encourage the use of unilateralism and the trend of using force or threat of using force on the part of the United States in its handling of international affairs, which will further increase the factors of instability in the world and relevant areas.

■ The practice of introducing the theater missile defense [TMD] system into the Asia-pacific region by making the TMD system part of the NMD system is unfavorable for the peace and security in the region. Recently, with joint efforts of relevant countries, some hot spots in the Asia-pacific region have seen lowering temperatures. In particular, the peace process on the Korean Peninsula has obtained a historical breakthrough. Introduction of the TMD system into the Asia-pacific region will only add new complications and confrontation factors to this region.[17]

05/15/2001: During the Chinese foreign ministry's regular bi-weekly briefing, spokesman Sun Yuxi spoke out against U.S. plans for an anti-missile defense system:

■ "This plan does not help the U.S. side and it also harms the interests of other countries. It will endanger strategic balance and stability, and will also trigger a new arms race in the world."

Despite U.S. Assistant Secretary of State James Kelly's recent attempts to soften China's opposition to National Missile Defense, China's opposition is resolute:

■ "Once you've invented a new spear, you of course will invent a new shield, and once you have invented a new shield, you invent new types of spears," he said. "It's always going on like that."

The spokesman said China was even more opposed to the Theater Missile Defense, especially if it were to cover Taiwan:

■ "(Inclusion of Taiwan) constitutes interference in China's internal affairs and will surely be met with firm opposition from the Chinese side. Since NMD is still in the process of being discussed, and has not been put in place, we will not talk about any concrete actions taken that would constitute any threat," said Sun.[18]

China, like most American adversaries, wants to retain the right to sell weapons—including missiles and weapons of mass destruction—to our less-powerful adversaries. While doing so, they object to our interference, even if it is by enforcing American law.

STATEMENT BY CHINESE FOREIGN MINISTRY OPPOSING U.S. IMPOSITION OF MISSILE PROLIFERATION SANCTIONS

The Chinese government has made solemn representations with the government of the United States over its decision to impose sanctions against the Chinese side, a spokesman for the Chinese Foreign Ministry said here Wednesday afternoon.

U.S. government decided, starting from September 1, to impose sanctions against the Chinese side under the pretext of the so-called export of missile-related items to Pakistan by the China Metallurgical Equipment Corporation (MECC). The Chinese side cannot but express strong indignation at and resolute opposition to the United States' hegemonic act of willfully imposing sanctions on other countries according to its domestic laws.

Over a period of time, the U.S. has repeatedly alleged that MECC was engaged in missile proliferation activities according to its so-called "intelligence information." In-depth investigations by the Chinese side indicate that MECC has never engaged in any activities as alleged by the United States and the U.S. allegation is groundless.

The U.S. side is bent on making the erroneous decision based on its wrong intelligence information, in disregard of the constructive position and the investigation results of the Chinese side. Such a U.S. move is totally groundless and irresponsible, which the Chinese side can never accept.

On the issue of non-proliferation, the Chinese policy is consistent and clear-cut. Last November, China and the United States announced respectively their policies on missile non-proliferation and Sino-U.S. cooperation on space launching. China has all along strictly fulfilled its own commitment. However, the U.S. side not only failed to honor its own commitment, but also decided to impose sanctions on China out of nowhere.

This cannot but make us doubt the sincerity of the United States in honoring the relevant bilateral understandings.

The improvement and development of Sino-U.S. relations is in the common interest of the two sides and calls for joint efforts. China strongly urges the U.S. side to immediately withdraw its wrong decision, so as to avoid any damage to Sino-U.S. cooperation in non-proliferation. Otherwise, the U.S. side should bear all the responsibilities for the consequences arising therefrom.[19]

China—and Russia too—have permanent seats on the UN Security Council, and with them, veto power over any UNSC resolutions.

They, along with France, use the UN as a restraint on the United States acting in its own interests. When we invaded Iraq in 2003, the PRC objected strenuously, demanding we return to the UN.

NATIONAL PEOPLE'S CONGRESS FOREIGN AFFAIRS COMMITTEE ISSUES STATEMENT ON THE MILITARY ACTIONS AGAINST IRAQ BY THE UNITED STATES AND OTHER COUNTRIES

21 March, 2003

On 20 March, the United States and other countries launched military actions against Iraq, and we express our serious anxiety about this matter.

As a permanent member of the UN Security Council, China has all the while dedicated itself to defend the unity, authority, and role of the UN Security Council; always maintained that the Iraqi issue should be resolved politically within the framework of the United Nations; demanded that the Iraqi government strictly, comprehensively, and conscientiously carry out the relevant resolutions of the Security Council and thoroughly destroys its weapons of mass destruction; and at the same time held that the sovereignty and territorial integrity of Iraq ought to be respected. Resolution 1441 adopted unanimously by the Security Council is an important basis for the political solution of the Iraqi issue. In order not to give up any gleam of hope for peace, China together with all the parties concerned has always made sustained efforts in this regard.

The Chinese people and the people of the world need peace. We have consistently dedicated ourselves to the protection of peace and stability in the world, maintained that international dispute should be settled through political means, and opposed the resort to force in international dispute.

The military actions against Iraq by the United States and other countries will lead to humanitarian disaster, result in casualties and property loss of the Iraqi people, and endanger regional peace and stability. We are deeply worried about the development of the situation. We strongly urge the countries concerned to comply with the wish of the international community, halt the military actions, and quickly return to the course of political solution.[20]

Hu Jintao's motto for China's emergence is "peaceful rise." Does that remind anyone of "stability"?

NINE

Putin's Russia

In November 2001, President Bush hosted Russian president Vladimir Putin at his ranch in Texas. It wasn't like Reagan hosting Gorbachev, a meeting of adversaries crafted to reduce tensions. It was the time President Bush famously said, "Well, in order for countries to come together, the first thing that must happen is leaders must make up their mind that they want this to happen. And the more I get to know President Putin, the more I get to see his heart and soul, and the more I know we can work together in a positive way."[1]

President Bush's optimism has proved unjustified, his judgment of Putin wrong. Putin is rebuilding Russia as an authoritarian neo-Soviet state. Putin's actions—such as building Iran's nuclear facilities (and his personal political party being enriched by Saddam Hussein's bribery in the UN Oil for Food program)—and words, tell the story better than any characterization can. Please read his words in the context of his personal biography. Putin is a former agent of the KGB who served in East Germany, perhaps the most oppressive of all the Soviet satellite states. He earned a black belt in judo, a

Japanese martial art whose central principle is to use an enemy's momentum and weight against him. That art takes form in his diplomacy.

Some of Putin's favorite themes: he denies that terrorists exist, defends Iran and its nuclear program, praises the influence of al Jazeera, and more, as illustrated by this recent interview he gave al Jazeera on a day he made a big speech and an even bigger media splash.

Here are excerpts from a February 10, 2007, interview Putin gave on al Jazeera:[2]

QUESTION: . . . Let me begin with one of the most pressing prob-lems—Iraq. What is your assessment of the situation in Iraq? Do you think what we are seeing there is civil war?

VLADIMIR PUTIN: We were against this from the outset. Our posi-tion of principle is that we always oppose the use of military means to resolve any of the problems in international affairs, all the more so without direct authorization from the UN Security Council, because this undermines the international-legal foundations of peace throughout the world. But what has happened has happened and we have to deal today with the reality of the situation. We will do all we can to work together with everyone involved in this process to help resolve this sit-uation.

The situation is very worrying, of course, and it is no exag-geration to say that it is indeed tragic. Saddam Hussein was executed just recently. I do not wish to comment on this at the moment. But what were the charges made against him? He was charged with carrying out reprisals against the residents of Shiite villages that resulted in the execution of around 148 people, and more in another location. Those were the kinds of figures cited, in any case. But since military operations began in Iraq, more than 3,000 Americans have been killed and the number of Iraqi civilians killed, according to various estimates, is already in the hundreds of thousands. Can we really compare these two situations?

Of course, we must reflect on how to find a way out of this situation. I think that unless the Iraqi people are given the right and possibility to decide their own future, it will not be possible to resolve this problem.

QUESTION: And what do you see as the solution?

VLADIMIR PUTIN: The solution is simple: strengthen Iraq's own capacity to ensure its security, withdraw the foreign contingent from Iraqi soil and give the Iraqi people the chance to decide their own future.

QUESTION: Can I ask you then what your view is of the new American strategy for Iraq that Mr. Bush announced recently, and will this strategy solve the problem?

VLADIMIR PUTIN: A new strategy, as we understand it, should involve a new approach to resolving this or that problem. If the strategy involves only increasing the numbers, we don't see anything new in it. When our American partners talk simply of boosting their military contingent, we do not consider this to be a new strategy. But that does not mean that there is nothing new in President Bush's initiatives. I think that there is something new in a point that was spoken about before but not cemented as the official line, namely, as I said just before, this issue of transferring full powers, above all in the areas of law enforcement and security, to the appropriate Iraqi departments and agencies. The U.S. president has spoken about this

publicly, it is reflected in his latest initiative, and if this is the
official line, we can say that this does represent something
new. But I think that it will work only if a date is set for the
withdrawal of the foreign contingent. This is because in any
conflict and in any country, people in the country have to
know by what date they need to be ready to take full responsibility for their country upon themselves. When there is no
clear date, when it is not clear at what point the country's
institutions need to have reached a certain level of development, responsibility ends up being placed on the foreign contingent. I think that a date should be set for the withdrawal of
the foreign troops.

QUESTION: Yes. Now, turning to another big issue—Iran. Mr.
President, you are in regular contact with the Iranian leadership. Have you received any positive signals from Tehran on
settling the Iranian nuclear issue?

VLADIMIR PUTIN: . . . . We know the position of our Iranian partners. We very much hope that they will also give consideration
to our recommendations. There are no questions or doubts on
the Iranian side as to the sincerity of our relations with Iran. All
of our action seeks to settle the confrontation over the Iranian
nuclear issue. We think that this would not take much. Iran
must address the concerns of [UN International Atomic Energy
Agency chief] Mr. El-Baradei and the organization he heads, but
we do not think that this need in any way infringe on Iran's plans
and right to develop peaceful nuclear technology.

QUESTION: As you know, Mr. El-Baradei recently proposed that
Iran stop its uranium enrichment activities simultaneously
with a lifting of sanctions against Tehran. Am I right in understanding that you support this initiative?

VLADIMIR PUTIN: Yes, we support it. We think it is a carefully
conceived and balanced initiative that does not harm Iran's
interests.

QUESTION: In your contacts with the Iranians, have you received
any positive signals about this initiative in particular?

VLADIMIR PUTIN: We have received the signal that Iran would
like to resolve this problem, but as to whether our Iranian partners are willing to respond positively to Mr. El-Baradei's proposals, we have not heard anything constructive on this
particular issue.

QUESTION: Russia's foreign minister, Mr. Lavrov, said a few days
ago that Washington had assured him that it did not have
plans for military intervention in Iran. Could you say that this
constitutes guarantees from the USA on this issue?

VLADIMIR PUTIN: This matter is one of the key issues on the
international agenda, and not only with regard to Iran. This
is a matter of security guarantees in the world in general and
the modern architecture of international relations. Can the
members of the international community feel that international law really does provide them with solid and reliable
protection today? Or are we going to make unilateral decisions not based on international law part of the practice of
international relations?

We very much hope that the assurances Mr. Lavrov
received from our American colleagues really do correspond to
reality. We think, and I hope, that is indeed the case.

But at the same time, I think that people in Iran and
throughout the entire world remember very well how events
developed in Iraq, which you asked me about at the start of
this interview. I would just like to remind you that we adopted

a resolution on Iraq in the autumn of 2002, and the IAEA noted that Iraq was cooperating actively with the organisation and positively assessed Iraq's efforts to develop this coopera- tion. Despite this, military operations began in the spring of 2003. This is the first point that raises concern.

Second, the new initiative on Iraq that you mentioned pro- vides for not only increasing the military contingent on Iraqi soil itself, but also for deploying aircraft carrying units in the region. Independent military experts say that this is not neces- sary for resolving the problem in Iraq.

Furthermore, a fairly large naval presence armed with mis- sile technology is already deployed in the Persian Gulf and is not being used for operations in Iraq. All of this together does raise questions and gives us some cause for concern.

QUESTION: The West, the USA, and Israel criticize Russia for its military and technical assistance to Iran, including in the field of nuclear energy. Do you plan to continue this cooperation despite the fuss it has caused?

VLADIMIR PUTIN: We are always being criticized for something. I know of no country that has not at some point or another been criticized for its foreign policy, if it is able to pursue an active and independent foreign policy in keeping with its national interests. Our foreign policy is highly balanced. We pursue our national interests, but at the same time we comply strictly with the Charter of the United Nations and with international law in general.

In this respect, I would like to say that our nuclear energy and military-technical cooperation with Iran is not in contra- diction with any international laws. We have not taken a sin- gle step that violates any of the international agreements relating to Iran. Our nuclear program, the program to build a nuclear power plant for electricity production at Bushehr is exclusively peaceful and is under the full control of IAEA inspectors. The inspectors have their verification equipment in place and are always present, and they have no claims to make against our program at Bushehr. We will continue to follow this same line in any future action. We are categorically opposed to the proliferation of nuclear weapons. It is not in our own national interests to even consider for a second allowing another country to acquire nuclear weapons. This would not contribute to strengthening world peace.

As for our military-technical cooperation, we cooperate in this area with many countries in the region and not just with Iran. We have been working with Iran for around forty years now, but this cooperation is very limited. We have made very few arms supplies to Iran. Our last supply was the delivery of mid-range air defense systems with a radius of thirty to fifty kilometers. This is a purely defensive weapons system and the supply of this kind of weapons system does not upset the balance of power in the region. Looking at arms supplies to the region as a whole, Russia supplies many times fewer arms to the Middle East than do a good number of other countries. I think that our actions are therefore fully justified. We act within the limits of international law, as I said. But as far as Iran goes, there is one other issue that I think we should not forget. We think that Iran should not be made to feel that it is surrounded by hostile forces. I think we must not push a country such as Iran and the Iranian people into a dead end, into some kind of trap. The Iranian people and leadership must realize that they do have friends in this world, that there are people ready to talk to them, and that there are people they can trust. We need to make them aware of this so as to create the atmosphere that will help us to resolve the most pressing problem we face with Iran—that of its nuclear problem.

QUESTION: .... Mr. President, a year ago, if you recall, you were asked your view of the Hamas victory in Palestinian parliamentary elections. Your response caused a big stir in the West at that time because you said that Russia had never considered Hamas a terrorist organization. Your decision to invite Hamas officials to Moscow caused even greater controversy. Do you now regret that position you took then?

VLADIMIR PUTIN: No, not at all. We have no regrets and on the contrary, we think that we were right to do what we did. The situation is very urgent today. I don't have time to make an analysis of all the events since the late 1940s that have brought the region to the state it is in today, and in any case, this interview is not the right moment for such a detailed analysis. But it is obvious that the situation is very complex and that there are many mutual claims, grievances and unresolved problems that have accumulated. Our position is that all the people living in this region have the right to statehood and to a safe existence. That is the first point.

Second, Hamas has used it own means to fight for its stated aims, and I am not certain that they have always been good means. But Hamas won the election. And we have always heard and still keep hearing calls from our European and American partners, to develop democracy....

Alright, say Hamas is driven underground, but the problems won't go underground, they will remain out in the open. We need to take another approach. After all, if Hamas is responsible for the Palestinian people's future, it will behave accordingly and will be simply forced to take the reality of the situation into account, and the reality is that the state of Israel exists. The reality is also that the international community and the entire world not only agrees with this but has cemented it in international agreements adopted by the United Nations.

I think that anyone can understand that if a political group claims the right to lead a people and a country, it cannot ignore the view of all of humanity, as expressed in agreements adopted by the world's universal international organization—the United Nations. It is my view therefore that we should of course work with Hamas to convince it of the need to recognize Israel's right of existence.

This is not easy of course, but it is better to work with people who have influence among their country's people and try to transform their position through negotiations than to pretend that they do not exist.

Is it possible to achieve such a shift in their views? Of course it is. Just remember one influential political leader in the Arab world—Yasser Arafat. There was a time, after all, when he was also viewed as a terrorist, but he ended up receiving the Nobel Peace Prize. This shows that change is possible. We just need to have patience and be willing to work together.

QUESTION: Mr. President, if you permit, I would like to look at more global issues now.

You reacted negatively to the U.S. decision to deploy elements of its missile defense system in some Eastern European countries. In taking these steps, are the Americans violating earlier agreements in this area?

VLADIMIR PUTIN: I cannot speak of violations of specific agreements, though this could be a matter for discussion at expert
level. I want to say that after the Berlin Wall came down, we
talked a lot and in great detail about the fact that we must
build a Europe without dividing lines. We also signed the
Treaty on Conventional Armed Forces in Europe.

We are complying with these limitations. But at the same
time, we see that new virtual "Berlin Walls" are being erected.
Instead of a common space, what we see instead is that this
"Berlin Wall" is simply being shifted further east and that new
bases are being established.

We are complying with all the arms limitation obligations
we have taken on, but our partners do not seem to feel bound
by these obligations. Many of them have not ratified this agreement, and this, of course, gives us some cause for concern.

QUESTION: Mr. President, continuing on this subject, does this
step taken by the USA require you to make changes to your
own military plans?

VLADIMIR PUTIN: Of course we are forced to take this situation
into account, because it is one matter when we hear talk of
political transformation of, say, NATO and another matter
when we see in reality that NATO's military infrastructure is
coming closer to our borders. Of course this forces us to
respond, and we are responding.

QUESTION: How?

VLADIMIR PUTIN: We are shaping our military doctrine accordingly and equipping our armed forces to address the new tasks
that emerge.

QUESTION: Many in the West see Russia's announcement that it
has unique missiles unlike any other in the world as some kind
of demonstration of its power. What do you say to this?

VLADIMIR PUTIN: They are right.

QUESTION: So this is a way of demonstrating Russia's strength?

VLADIMIR PUTIN: Of course.

RESPONSE: But this sometimes provokes a negative reaction towards Russia in the West.

VLADIMIR PUTIN: It provokes a negative reaction among people who do not realise the meaning of what is taking place. What is the meaning of what is taking place? This is a complex issue, but I will try to give a brief explanation.

From the point of view of stability in this or that region or in the world in general, the balance of power is the main achievement of these past decades and indeed of the whole history of humanity. It is one of the most important conditions for maintaining global stability and security. When we see that our partners are developing new weapons systems and bringing their military infrastructure closer to our borders, we are forced to make some kind of response. Take the plans to create a missile defense system, for example. They change the balance of power. If one side puts this system in place, the other side might feel less sure of its security, and this also changes the balance of power. Faced with this situation, we are forced to make a response, at the very minimum an asymmetric response. If we decide not to build our own missile defense system in response then we must design a system that will be able to penetrate the missile defenses being built by our partners. This is all very logical and clear, and this is precisely what we are doing.

QUESTION: Following the gas crisis with Ukraine at the start of last year and the problems with Belarus at the beginning of this year, many in the West have been saying that Russia is using its energy resources as a weapon for political blackmail.

How do you plan to build your future relations with foreign consumers of your energy resources?

VLADIMIR PUTIN: I not only think but I am certain that statements of this kind have no grounds in reality. They are either a line of attack used by those who wish our country no good, or are a means of unfair competition. No other country, after all, is expected to accept non-market relations and offer preferential conditions to other countries, and we do not understand why we should be expected to do so. Our action aims solely at establishing exclusively market-based relations with our partners, both with consumers and transit countries. We are not proposing anything else. Moreover, I can give you an example that very clearly illustrates what I have just said and that shows that this really is the foundation of our energy policy.

Our political relations with the Baltic States could certainly be better, but nonetheless, we reached an agreement with them three or four years ago about introducing market prices and we signed agreements on a gradual transition to these prices. Since then, we have continued subsidizing their economies by supplying cheap energy resources, but gradually raising the price. This has had no impact on our political relations with these countries. They were not very good to begin with and, unfortunately, they remain on the whole not very good today. We have never used energy as an instrument in our relations with these countries.

Still at the beginning of last year, Latvia was paying only 60 percent of the market price for, say, natural gas from Russia, and it was only this year that we gradually introduced market prices in our dealings with Latvia. We are taking exactly the same approach with all our other partners.

When we see here and there criticism of Russia's wish to establish market relations with its partners become all-out hysteria it is really just covering for political aims with regard to Russia. It is really in this case a means of trying to influence Russia.

QUESTION: There is a lot of talk in the West about violations of human rights and freedoms in Russia. You have come in for a lot of criticism personally in this respect. How do you react to this criticism?

VLADIMIR PUTIN: I see it in much the same way as I see the criticism of our energy policy. I think that to a considerable extent it is being used as a means of influencing Russian internal politics and I think that some countries are using this kind of demagogy as a means to pursue their own foreign policy goals in Russia.

I do not really understand why some of our partners are trying to return to a situation where they see themselves as cleverer and more civilized and think that they have the right to impose their standards on others. Let them go to China and try managing its more than 1.5 billion people. I doubt they would do it better than Mr. Hu Jintao. The thing to remember is that standards that are imposed from outside, including in the Middle East, rather than being a product of a society's natural internal development, lead to tragic consequences, and the best example of this is Iraq.

QUESTION: Mr. President, you are about to make the first visit by a Russian president to the countries of the Persian Gulf. This region has so far been on the margins of Russian foreign policy and foreign economic policy. What are your forecasts for the future?

VLADIMIR PUTIN: This situation arose because during the Soviet
years there were ideological barriers and contradictions that
got in the way of developing relations with these countries.
The fact that these barriers have disappeared is one of the positive results to come out of the last decade or fifteen years.
There are no countries in the Arab world now with whom we
have contradictions of any kind. This gives us the chance to
develop our relations with all countries in the region, including the Gulf states. We do indeed hope that the resources
these countries possess, above all the financial resources,
could be used in the growing Russian economy. There are no
obstacles to this. One of the aims of my visit is to reaffirm the
high status of the intergovernmental relations between our
countries today and find ways of developing these relations in
the economic sphere.

QUESTION: I am happy to recall that there will soon be an Arab-
language channel in Russia that will show events taking place in
Russia from Russia's point of view. How do you think this will
help to build bridges between the Arab countries and Russia?

VLADIMIR PUTIN: Building bridges was the whole reason we
decided to go ahead with these plans. Of course this step
should help to develop direct relations in the information field
between Russia and the Arab world, between your people and
our people, who have a long-standing interest in and love for
Arab culture.

QUESTION: Mr. President, among ordinary people in the Arab
countries there is a certain nostalgia for the Soviet Union.
Many people think that your foreign policy will restore Russia
to the place the Soviet Union once held. What would you say
to them?

VLADIMIR PUTIN: I want to say that Russia does not seek super-power status. Russia does not seek conflict with anyone. But Russia knows its worth. We will work towards creating a multipolar world. We do not want to return to the era of confrontation between opposing blocs. We do not want to split the world into different military and political groupings. But Russia does have enough potential to influence the formation of the new world order and to ensure that the future architecture of international relations is balanced and takes the interests of all members of the international community into account.

Russia seeks no new power, only that of shaping the "new world order." Its natural gas blackmail of its former satellites is only business. (Just as henchman Tessio, being taken off for execution because he betrayed Godfather Michael Corleone, said, "Tell Michael it was only business. I always liked him.")

Russia is Iran's partner. Its sales of missile defense systems to Iran—deployed to protect the Iranian regime and its nuclear program—are all innocent, we are told. And Hamas and Hizballah aren't terrorists. This is our "friend" Mr. Putin in action.

That same day, February 10, 2007, Putin gave a speech in Munich in which he renewed the Soviets' Cold War call for arms control, preventing weapons from being placed in space and sounded much like one of his forebears: Leonid Brezhnev. The following are excerpts from the speech:[3]

...It is well known that international security comprises much more than issues relating to military and political stability. It involves the stability of the global economy, overcoming poverty, economic security and developing a dialogue between civilizations.

This universal, indivisible character of security is expressed as the basic principle that "security for one is security for all." As Franklin D. Roosevelt said during the first few days that the Second World War was breaking out: "When peace has been broken anywhere, the peace of all countries everywhere is in danger."

These words remain topical today. Incidentally, the theme of our conference—global crises, global responsibility—exemplifies this.

Only two decades ago the world was ideologically and economically divided and it was the huge strategic potential of two superpowers that ensured global security.

This global stand-off pushed the sharpest economic and social problems to the margins of the international community's and the world's agenda. And, just like any war, the Cold War left us with live ammunition, figuratively speaking. I am referring to ideological stereotypes, double standards and other typical aspects of Cold War bloc thinking.

The unipolar world that had been proposed after the Cold War did not take place either.

The history of humanity certainly has gone through unipolar periods and seen aspirations to world supremacy. And what hasn't happened in world history?

However, what is a unipolar world? However one might embellish this term, at the end of the day it refers to one type of situation, namely one centre of authority, one centre of force, one centre of decision-making.

It is world in which there is one master, one sovereign. And at the end of the day this is pernicious not only for all those within this system, but also for the sovereign itself because it destroys itself from within.

And this certainly has nothing in common with democracy. Because, as you know, democracy is the power of the majority in light of the interests and opinions of the minority.

Incidentally, Russia—we—are constantly being taught about democracy. But for some reason those who teach us do not want to learn themselves. I consider that the unipolar model is not only unacceptable but also impossible in today's world. And this is not only because if there was individual leadership in today's—and precisely in today's—world, then the military, political and economic resources would not suffice. What is even more important is that the model itself is flawed because at its basis there is and can be no moral foundations for modern civilization.

Along with this, what is happening in today's world—and we just started to discuss this—is a tentative to introduce precisely this concept into international affairs, the concept of a unipolar world. And with which results?

Unilateral and frequently illegitimate actions have not resolved any problems. Moreover, they have caused new human tragedies and created new centres of tension. Judge for yourselves: wars as well as local and regional conflicts have not diminished. Mr. Teltschik mentioned this very gently. And no less people perish in these conflicts—even more are dying than before. Significantly more, significantly more!

Today we are witnessing an almost uncontained hyper use of force—military force—in international relations, force that is plunging the world into an abyss of permanent conflicts. As a result we do not have sufficient strength to find a comprehensive solution to any one of these conflicts. Finding a political settlement also becomes impossible.

We are seeing a greater and greater disdain for the basic principles of international law. And independent legal norms are, as a matter of fact, coming increasingly closer to one state's legal system. One state and, of course, first and foremost the United States, has overstepped its national borders in every way. This is visible in the economic, political, cultural and educational policies it imposes on other nations. Well, who likes this? Who is happy about this?

In international relations we increasingly see the desire to resolve a given question according to so-called issues of political expediency, based on the current political climate. And of course this is extremely dangerous. It results in the fact that no one feels safe. I want to emphasize this—no one feels safe! Because no one can feel that international law is like a stone wall that will protect them. Of course such a policy stimulates an arms race.

The force's dominance inevitably encourages a number of countries to acquire weapons of mass destruction. Moreover, significantly new threats—though they were also well-known before—have appeared, and today threats such as terrorism have taken on a global character.

I am convinced that we have reached that decisive moment when we must seriously think about the architecture of global security.

And we must proceed by searching for a reasonable balance between the interests of all participants in the international dialogue. Especially since the international landscape is so varied and changes so quickly—changes in light of the dynamic development in a whole number of countries and regions.

Madam Federal Chancellor already mentioned this. The combined GDP measured in purchasing power parity of countries such as India and China is already greater than that of the United States. And a similar calculation with the GDP of the BRIC countries—Brazil, Russia, India and China—surpasses the cumulative GDP of the EU. And according to experts this gap will only increase in the future.

There is no reason to doubt that the economic potential of the new centers of global economic growth will inevitably be converted into political influence and will strengthen multipolarity.

In connection with this the role of multilateral diplomacy is significantly increasing. The need for principles such as openness, transparency and predictability in politics is uncontested and the use of force should be a really exceptional measure, comparable to using the death penalty in the judicial systems of certain states.

However, today we are witnessing the opposite tendency, namely a situation in which countries that forbid the death penalty even for murderers and other, dangerous criminals are airily participating in military operations that are difficult to consider legitimate. And as a matter of fact, these conflicts are killing people—hundreds and thousands of civilians!

But at the same time the question arises of whether we should be indifferent and aloof to various internal conflicts inside countries, to authoritarian regimes, to tyrants, and to the proliferation of weapons of mass destruction? As a matter of fact, this was also at the centre of the question that our dear colleague Mr. Lieberman asked the Federal Chancellor. If I correctly understood your question (addressing Mr. Lieberman), then of course it is a serious one! Can we be indifferent observers in view of what is happening? I will try to answer your question as well: of course not.

But do we have the means to counter these threats? Certainly we do. It is sufficient to look at recent history. Did not our country have a peaceful transition to democracy? Indeed, we witnessed a peaceful transformation of the Soviet regime—a peaceful transformation! And what a regime! With what a number of weapons, including nuclear weapons! Why should we start bombing and shooting now at every available opportunity? Is it the case when without the threat of mutual destruction we do not have enough political culture, respect for democratic values and for the law?

I am convinced that the only mechanism that can make decisions about using military force as a last resort is the Charter of the United Nations. And in connection with this, either I did not understand what our colleague, the Italian Defense Minister, just said or what he said was inexact. In any case, I understood that the use of force can only be legitimate when the decision is taken by NATO, the EU, or the UN. If he really does think so, then we have different points of view. Or I didn't hear correctly. The use of force can only be considered legitimate if the decision is sanctioned by the UN. And we do not need to substitute NATO or the EU for the UN. When the UN will truly unite the forces of the international community and can really react to events in various countries, when we will leave behind this disdain for international law, then the situation will be able to change. Otherwise the situation will simply result in a dead end, and the number of serious mistakes will be multiplied. Along with this, it is necessary to make sure that international law have a universal character both in the conception and application of its norms.

And one must not forget that democratic political actions necessarily go along with discussion and a laborious decision-making process.

Dear ladies and gentlemen!

The potential danger of the destabilization of international relations is connected with obvious stagnation in the disarmament issue.

Russia supports the renewal of dialogue on this important question. It is important to conserve the international legal framework relating to weapons destruction and therefore ensure continuity in the process of reducing nuclear weapons.

Together with the United States of America we agreed to reduce our nuclear strategic missile capabilities to up to 1700–2000 nuclear warheads by 31 December 2012. Russia intends to strictly fulfill the obligations it has taken on. We hope that our partners will also act in a transparent way and will refrain from laying aside a couple of hundred superfluous nuclear warheads for a rainy day. And if today the new American Defense Minister declares that the United States will not hide these superfluous weapons in warehouse or, as one might say, under a pillow or under the blanket, then I suggest that we all rise and greet this declaration standing. It would be a very important declaration.

Russia strictly adheres to and intends to further adhere to the Treaty on the Non-Proliferation of Nuclear Weapons as well as the multilateral supervision regime for missile technologies. The principles incorporated in these documents are universal ones.

In connection with this I would like to recall that in the 1980s the USSR and the United States signed an agreement on destroying a whole range of small- and medium-range missiles but these documents do not have a universal character.

Today many other countries have these missiles, including the Democratic People's Republic of Korea, the Republic of Korea, India, Iran, Pakistan and Israel. Many countries are working on these systems and plan to incorporate them as part of their weapons arsenals. And only the United States and Russia bear the responsibility to not create such weapons systems.

It is obvious that in these conditions we must think about ensuring our own security.

At the same time, it is impossible to sanction the appearance of new, destabilizing high-tech weapons. Needless to say it refers to measures to prevent a new area of confrontation, especially in outer space. Star wars is no longer a fantasy—it is a reality. In the middle of the 1980s our American partners were already able to intercept their own satellite.

In Russia's opinion, the militarization of outer space could have unpredictable consequences for the international community, and provoke nothing less than the beginning of a nuclear era. And we have come forward more than once with initiatives designed to prevent the use of weapons in outer space.

Today I would like to tell you that we have prepared a project for an agreement on the prevention of deploying weapons in outer space. And in the near future it will be sent to our partners as an official proposal. Let's work on this together.

Plans to expand certain elements of the anti-missile defense system to Europe cannot help but disturb us. Who needs the next step of what would be, in this case, an inevitable arms race? I deeply doubt that Europeans themselves do.

Missile weapons with a range of about five to eight thousand kilometres that really pose a threat to Europe do not exist in any of the so-called problem countries. And in the near future and prospects, this will not happen and is not even foreseeable. And any hypothetical launch of, for example, a North Korean rocket to American territory through Western Europe obviously contradicts the laws of ballistics. As we say in Russia, it would be like using the right hand to reach the left ear.

And here in Germany I cannot help but mention the pitiable condition of the Treaty on Conventional Armed Forces in Europe.

The Adapted Treaty on Conventional Armed Forces in Europe was signed in 1999. It took into account a new geopolitical reality, namely the elimination of the Warsaw bloc. Seven years have passed and only four states have ratified this document, including the Russian Federation.

NATO countries openly declared that they will not ratify this treaty, including the provisions on flank restrictions (on deploying a certain number of armed forces in the flank zones), until Russia removed its military bases from Georgia and Moldova. Our army is leaving Georgia, even according to an accelerated schedule. We resolved the problems we had with our Georgian colleagues, as everybody knows. There are still 1,500 servicemen in Moldova that are carrying out peacekeeping operations and protecting warehouses with ammunition left over from Soviet times. We constantly discuss this issue with Mr Solana and he knows our position. We are ready to further work in this direction.

But what is happening at the same time? Simultaneously the so-called flexible frontline American bases with up to five thousand men in each. It turns out that NATO has put its frontline forces on our borders, and we continue to strictly fulfil the treaty obligations and do not react to these actions at all.

I think it is obvious that NATO expansion does not have any relation with the modernization of the Alliance itself or with ensuring security in Europe. On the contrary, it represents a serious provocation that reduces the level of mutual trust. And we have the right to ask: against whom is this expansion intended? And what happened to the assurances our western partners made after the dissolution of the Warsaw Pact? Where are those declarations today? No one even remembers them. But I will allow myself to remind this audience what was said. I would like to quote the speech of NATO General Secretary Mr. Woerner in Brussels on 17 May 1990. He said at the time that: "the fact that we are ready not to place a NATO army outside of German territory gives the Soviet Union a firm security guarantee." Where are these guarantees?

The stones and concrete blocks of the Berlin Wall have long been distributed as souvenirs. But we should not forget that the fall of the Berlin Wall was possible thanks to a historic choice— one that was also made by our people, the people of Russia—a choice in favor of democracy, freedom, openness and a sincere partnership with all the members of the big European family.

And now they are trying to impose new dividing lines and walls on us—these walls may be virtual but they are nevertheless dividing, ones that cut through our continent. And is it possible that we will once again require many years and decades, as well as several generations of politicians, to dissemble and dismantle these new walls?

Dear ladies and gentlemen!

We are unequivocally in favor of strengthening the regime of non-proliferation. The present international legal principles allow us to develop technologies to manufacture nuclear fuel for peaceful purposes. And many countries with all good reasons want to create their own nuclear energy as a basis for their energy independence. But we also understand that these technologies can be quickly transformed into nuclear weapons.

This creates serious international tensions. The situation surrounding the Iranian nuclear program acts as a clear example. And if the international community does not find a reasonable solution for resolving this conflict of interests, the world will continue to suffer similar, destabilizing crises because there are more threshold countries than simply Iran. We both know this. We are going to constantly fight against the threat of the proliferation of weapons of mass destruction.

Last year Russia put forward the initiative to establish international centres for the enrichment of uranium. We are open to the possibility that such centres not only be created in Russia, but also in other countries where there is a legitimate basis for using civil nuclear energy. Countries that want to develop their nuclear energy could guarantee that they will receive fuel through direct participation in these centres. And the centres would, of course, operate under strict IAEA supervision.

The latest initiatives put forward by American president George W. Bush are in conformity with the Russian proposals. I consider that Russia and the USA are objectively and equally interested in strengthening the regime of the non-proliferation of weapons of mass destruction and their deployment. It is precisely our countries, with leading nuclear and missile capabilities, that must act as leaders in developing new, stricter non-proliferation measures. Russia is ready for such work. We are engaged in consultations with our American friends. . . .

In conclusion I would like to note the following. We very often—and personally, I very often—hear appeals by our partners, including our European partners, to the effect that Russia should play an increasingly active role in world affairs.

In connection with this I would allow myself to make one small remark. It is hardly necessary to incite us to do so. Russia is a country with a history that spans more than a thousand years and has practically always used the privilege to carry out an independent foreign policy.

We are not going to change this tradition today. At the same time, we are well aware of how the world has changed and we have a realistic sense of our own opportunities and potential. And of course we would like to interact with responsible and independent partners with whom we could work together in constructing a fair and democratic world order that would ensure security and prosperity not only for a select few, but for all.

Thank you for your attention.

Putin's words still echo the Cold War. Defensive systems—such as the U.S. anti-missile defense now being built—are what "destabilizes" the world. Russia is only innocent, seeking reductions in arms. In truth, Putin is playing the Cold War game very well. He has a weak hand, but he's playing it very well.

Putin's addresses to the Russians are stronger. He plays to the international media too, but his words are directed at Russian nationalists. Below is part of Putin's Annual Address to the Federal Assembly of the Russian Federation on May 10, 2006, at the Kremlin:

I point out that our defense spending as a share of GDP is comparable or slightly less than in the other nuclear powers, France or Britain, for example. In terms of absolute figures, and we all know that in the end it is absolute figures that count, our defense spending is half that of the countries I mentioned, and bears no comparison at all with the defense spending figures in the United States. Their defense budget in absolute figures is almost twenty-five times bigger than Russia's. This is what in defense is referred to as "their home—their fortress." And good on them, I say. Well done!

But this means that we also need to build our home and make it strong and well protected. We see, after all, what is going on in the world. The wolf knows who to eat, as the saying goes. It knows who to eat and is not about to listen to anyone, it seems.

CNN reported in July 2006 that "during a joint news conference Saturday in St. Petersburg, Bush said he raised concerns about democracy in Russia during a frank discussion with the Russian leader." CNN quotes President Bush as saying, "I talked about my desire to promote institutional change in parts of the world, like Iraq where there's a free press and free religion, and I told him that a lot of people in our country would hope that Russia would do the same." Putin's response is: "We certainly would not want to have the same kind of democracy that they have in Iraq, quite honestly."[4] Or any other kind, for that matter.

Putin is not the only representative of the "new Russia" who is worth reading. Here is a selection of others.

The following is a selection of quotes from articles published in the February 28 editions of Russian newspapers, as available to the BBC on February 27, 2006:[5]

Progress in Russian-Iranian talks

- Rossiyskaya Gazeta [government newspaper]: Russia has far more reasons than the USA and Europe to fear the emergence of an aggressive, nuclear-armed Islamic superpower. The degree of concern is inversely proportional to the distance ("flying time," if you like) between the countries! For Russia Iran truly is the NEAR East. If we turn our back on the seething mass of Islamic fundamentalism, we could get burnt.[6]

- It is precisely because of its closeness to Iran that Russia is obliged to follow an extremely circumspect policy—the degree of circumspection is also inversely proportional to the distance!... But the most important point is this: at the moment the Islamists' hatred is channelled against Israel and the USA, which serve, objectively, as lightning conductors for Russia....[7]

- *Komsomolskaya Pravda*, [a popular tabloid controlled by businessman Vladimir Potanin:] The visit to Iran by Rosatom [Federal Agency for Atomic Agency] head Sergey Kiriyenko has proved successful.... The USA has been threatening to push international sanctions against Iran through the Security Council. If that were to happen, Russia could lose lucrative, billion-dollar contracts with its southern neighbour.[8]

- "The establishment of a joint venture could resolve this complex problem. Now, theoretically, there should be reliable control of the Iranian nuclear programme...."[9]

- [From *Krasnaya Zvezda* [Defense Ministry newspaper:] "Despite the Iranian side's agreement in principle to the Russian proposal for the establishment of a joint venture on Russian territory to meet all Iran's needs for nuclear fuel, tension in the negotiating process remains high...."[10]

Putin's Russia befriends terrorists, laying a smoke cloud around them, treating them as not quite friends, but clearly not enemies. It is the Soviet tactic: to help any nation or group that is the enemy of the United States.

Talking to Hamas

Moscow-based daily newspaper *Noskovskiy Komsomolets*, February 28, 2006:

■ "...Russian agitprop may now do its utmost to protect the
Kremlin from accusations of double standards. We can talk to
the Hamas terrorists, can't we, because they won a nationwide
and democratic election? This explanation is quite ingenious,
but unconvincing all the same. In 1997 Maskhadov also won
a nationwide election. But this did not stop Moscow proclaiming him an outlaw after a while. Alas, double standards
are an inalienable part of the political game. In real life, even
with the best intentions, it is not always possible to follow
noble slogans. This, apparently, is the one lesson that can be
learnt from the present stage of the Middle East tragedy."[11]

*Putin's support for terrorists is not new. He's been defending Hamas
and Hizballah for years. A few examples:*

Washington Post, February 1, 2006

MOSCOW, Jan. 31—Russian president Vladimir Putin described
the electoral victory of the radical Islamic group Hamas in the
Palestinian elections as "a big blow to American efforts in the
Middle East, a very serious blow," but he said Russia would not support any efforts to cut off financial assistance to the Palestinians.

"Our position on Hamas is different from that of the United
States and Western Europe," said Putin, speaking at an annual
news conference in the Kremlin. "The Russian Foreign Ministry
has never regarded Hamas as a terrorist organization. But this
does not mean that we totally approve and support everything that
Hamas has done."

"I think if we want to deal with complex global problems, we only have to do this together," he said. "And we should not invite certain participants in some or other process to make cats' paws of them," using an expression that means to toy with someone. "We should sit down together and listen and hear what others say, and we should make concerted decisions."

"There are devoted Sovietologists who do not understand what is happening in our country, do not understand the changing world," Putin said. "They deserve a very brief response: 'To hell with you.'"

"It is my deep conviction that in the post-Soviet space, in conditions of developing economies, strengthening statehood, in conditions of the formation of federalism, we need strong presidential power."[12]

By supporting terrorists, Putin believes Russia serves as a counterweight to the U.S.'s influence. Or is he seeking to use the terrorists to further Russian interests by tying down the U.S. in the Middle East?

PUTIN: HAMAS NOT A TERROR ORGANIZATION

Russian president tells press conference in Madrid he intends on inviting group leaders to Moscow in near future; Hamas official says group would accept invitation

Russian president Vladimir Putin said during a press conference in Madrid Thursday that he intends on inviting the leaders of the Palestinian terror group to Moscow, Itar-Tass news agency said.

Hamas politburo Khaled Mashaal welcomed the Russian initiative, saying group representatives will travel to Moscow should Putin address an official invitation.

"If an invitation is addressed we will accept it. We welcome the courageous Russian position and the declarations of Mr.

Putin...in which he does not classify us a terror organization," AFP quoted Mashaal as saying.

He added that Russia's position "will lead to a certain equilibrium" in international relations, especially that "America's influence has started to wane because of numerous impasses in which the American administration is entangled."

Putin was quoted as telling a joint press conference with Spanish prime minister Jose Luis Rodriguez Zapatero in Madrid, where he was on a visit, that "Russia is maintaining contacts with the Hamas organization and intends in the near future to invite the leadership of this organization to Moscow."

Putin reiterated that Russia does not consider Hamas a terrorist organization, and urged the global community to work with a Hamas-led Palestinian government.

"Hamas has arrived at the doors of power through legitimate elections," Putin said. "We must respect the Palestinian people and we have to look for solutions for the Palestinian people, for the international community, and also for Israel. Contacts with Hamas must continue," he added.[13]

Putin Speaking to Russian Press

Putin's answers to questions from the Russian media following a visit to the Middle East:

PETROV (ITAR-TASS): Russia has always had a presence in one way or another in the Middle East. Was this visit a continuation of those past traditions, or does it signal a new direction in Russia's policy in the region?

VLADIMIR PUTIN: It continues past traditions and at the same time, it expands our contacts in the region. During the Soviet years, we had fairly cool relations with Saudi Arabia and Qatar, and even with Jordan our relations were not as good as they could have been. The situation has changed immensely over recent years. We are now developing active ties with these countries and the time has come to cement and build on these results. I am very happy with the outcome of this visit. We have not just reviewed the results of our work over recent years but have also outlined joint steps for continuing to develop our relations in the future.

We have signed a number of agreements, which I would divide into two categories. First, there are the agreements that strengthen the legal foundation for our cooperation with these countries, and second, there are the agreements on carrying out specific projects. These projects include plans for work together in the high-technology sector, in aviation and space. We have also agreed on a project that would see the assembly of Russian motor vehicles here in Jordan.

We place great importance on coordinating our work on the global energy markets. In this respect, Saudi Arabia and Qatar are both priority partners.

Our contacts have also been very productive in terms of developing humanitarian ties. There has always been great interest in the culture of the Middle East in Russia, and our country has an excellent school of Arab studies. We spoke about this during our meetings. And finally, here in Jordan we had the opportunity of visiting the River Jordan. I think that the Russian Orthodox Church will have good facilities here for welcoming pilgrims. All of this together gives me reason to say that this visit has been a success.

O. OSIPOV (RIA-NOVOSTI): I would like to come back to the events of a few days ago. Your speech in Munich is still being much discussed. What prompted you to make such frank statements right at this moment? Why did you choose this time to set out your views on the situation in the world? Judging by the publications and responses to your words, your colleagues in the West consider your statements to be confrontational.

VLADIMIR PUTIN: The theme of the conference in Munich was "Global crisis—global responsibility." For many years now, for more than a decade, we have been listening to what our partners say on issues in various areas. Of course, it is true that statements of the kind that were made also have a bilateral dimension in terms of Russian-U.S. relations. We have seen many positive developments in our relations with the United States, but we are becoming increasingly convinced that often the action taken by our partners in different areas, and the instruments they use with regard to Russia, pursue the sole purpose of furthering their own interests with regard to our country.

We take a patient and tolerant approach to this kind of policy, but we have the impression that some of our partners do not understand us and are turning up the pressure more and more. Things have got to the stage where the non-existent Russian threat has started being used as a pretext for getting the U.S. Congress to increase defense spending—defense spending that will be used to carry out military operations in Iraq and Afghanistan, and to build an expensive missile defense system.

But these are not our problems and they are not connected to Russia in any way. We simply do not understand the need to play the anti-Russian card in resolving domestic political issues. Personally, I have come to the conclusion that it does not matter what we do—provide answers and explanations or simply sit tight and keep silent—there will always be someone who comes up with some pretext for attacking Russia. In this situation, it is better to simply be frank and direct in setting out our views.

But I also want to point out that what was said in Munich has been said before in one form or another in direct discussions with our American colleagues. There was nothing unexpected or out of the ordinary for them in what I said. I was pleased that representatives of the U.S. administration and the parliament, U.S. senators, in particular, where sitting in the front row in the conference hall in Munich, because I would not have wanted to make such statements in their absence, behind their back.

These issues are being discussed not only in Russia but in places all around the world, and this has been the case for a long time now. The difference is that some countries do indeed take a very blunt and confrontational approach, actually, insulting the United States and its leadership, and I think this is counterproductive and unacceptable in general. Other countries say the same things, but only in whispers, only behind the scenes. I think that Russia is a country that should not act behind the scenes nor have a grudge against anyone, but on the contrary, should state its views frankly, openly and honestly. I think that it is through this approach that we can open the road for normal, honest and candid dialogue, and I think that there are people in the United States who will hear our voice and will try to build relations with us based on friendly equality and without a lecturing tone.

Finally and most importantly, I am deeply convinced that what I said is the truth, and that the situation I referred to really is what is happening in the world. I have no illusions or hopes that everything will suddenly change overnight after my speech in Munich. Of course this will not be the case. But let us remember that here in Jordan we visited the biblical lands, and in the Bible it says that, "In the beginning was the Word." I believe that gradually we will see correct, needed and positive changes in the world, and that we will build a fairer and more democratic world, working together with the direct participation of our American partners.

V. TEREKHOV (INTERFAX): What kind of response do you expect from your foreign colleagues and partners? After all, you practically said that the balance and the system of relations in the world have been upset....

VLADIMIR PUTIN: This has long since been the case. We did not build a new world order but for the most part just went on living in the conditions of a bipolar system based on confrontation between the two big superpowers and their camps, and we did not build a new and democratic world order. My hope is, as I just said, that my frank and honest words have been heard. As I said, this is something everyone is talking about, only behind the scenes, and I decided to speak about it openly and directly....

One of the most powerful cliques in Soviet society was the military industrialists. When the Soviet empire fell apart, they suffered huge losses of wealth and status. Putin is aiming to restore their financial wealth and status in return for their political support.

QUESTION (NEZAVISIMAYA GAZETA): You have said nothing during this visit about military cooperation, but the Russian dele-
gation included representatives of the Russian defense
industry. Could you say a few words about cooperation in this
area with the Arab countries?

VLADIMIR PUTIN: Yes, our cooperation in this area is showing
good development and we are setting new records all the time
for sales volumes. This is a natural process. There is fierce
competition in the world today on these markets and Russia
has had some very good and visible results in this sector.

   We would like to consolidate our presence on markets
where we are already established, but we also want to expand
markets for selling our high-technology military goods. We did
indeed hold very productive talks on these issues and we have
reached a number of agreements.

   But I must point out that military-technical cooperation is
a very sensitive area and we can really only talk about concrete
deals once the contracts have been signed. We have not signed
any contracts as yet, but I have reason to believe that the
agreements we have reached with our partners have every
chance of being implemented. Once actual contracts and
agreements have been signed, you will be informed. The
agreements I refer to concern our traditional areas of cooperation: high-technology equipment, aviation, light arms, air
defense systems—offers are on the table in all of these areas,
but now it is a matter of choosing what is best suited to our
partners' needs.

QUESTION: You discussed with your partners, and perhaps also
with Mahmoud Abbas, the idea of holding a big conference on
the Middle East. What was their reaction to this idea? Also, I

know that there were objections at one time to the idea of Iran taking part. Was something said about this, and is it realistic for Iran to take part?

VLADIMIR PUTIN: If we are talking about achieving a comprehensive settlement it would probably not be right to leave someone outside these negotiations. But we are not stubbornly going to push just our initiative. We work in other formats—in the "Quartet" and directly with our partners in the Middle East.

We think this initiative is a good idea, but we are not obsessed with it. We are aware of the view of a number of our friends in the Arab world who think that it would be good to know first exactly what outcome the conference hopes to achieve. But if we knew the outcome, we would perhaps not even have to hold a conference in the first place. It would be enough to just sit down and sign everything straight away. We think that the conference could be a good idea to get this cooperation process moving. But at the same time, I have every reason to think that our work within the "Quartet" will result very soon in real progress in the settlement process.

Putin—who matured and thrived in the atheist Soviet era—speaks as a religious man. Who knew?

A. GAMOV (KOMSOMOLSKAYA PRAVDA): What did you feel and what were your impressions after visiting the holy river and site where Jesus Christ was baptized?

VLADIMIR PUTIN: First of all, the setting itself makes a strong impression. I don't know about you, but personally, right from the start, I had the feeling that I was really here in the biblical lands. There were two main aspects to my thoughts and impressions. First, of course, is the spiritual aspect. It's hard for me to comment on this because these are very personal feelings and I don't think I need describe them in detail for you and your colleagues. Second, there are the pragmatic considerations. As you know, the King of Jordan and the Prince, who is responsible for developing this site, have given Russia a hectare of land right on the banks of the River Jordan, close to the site where Christ was baptised. I would like to appeal to our business organizations to help the Russian Orthodox Church to build a guest house here for Russian pilgrims. I think this work could be done quite quickly.[14]

TEN

Kim Jong-il's North Korea

North Korea would be a comic opera nation were it not for its nuclear weapons and missiles capable of delivering them. China controls North Korea—the North Koreans depending almost entirely on China for food and fuel—but Kim Jong-il's character is such that the Chinese control may be unreliable in time of crisis. What else can one say about North Korea, whose only export commodities are missiles and counterfeit U.S. currency? His missiles threaten Japan and will soon be able to reach the Western U.S. Kim is not a comic figure. His capacity to counterfeit U.S. currency—if used more effectively—could affect the international value of our dollar. How dangerous is he? Let Kim speak for himself. This is a man who claims to have made eighteen consecutive holes-in-one the first time he played golf.

Excerpts from Kim Jong-il's _Selected Works_, extracted by the NDFSK (National Democratic

Front of South Korea) Mission in Pyongyang:

- The imperialists are now making frantic efforts to embellish capitalism and to slander socialism. In essence, however, capitalist society is an exploitative society ruled by the capitalist class; only socialist society is a genuinely popular society where the masses lead a worthy life on an equal basis as the masters of the state and society. This is an indisputable, established fact. The essential superiority of socialism over capitalism is that socialist society meets in full the intrinsic requirements of social beings to live and develop independently and creatively on an equal basis.

  Capitalist society is not by any means a rich and prosperous society as the imperialists claim, but a society where the rich get ever richer and the poor get ever poorer. In capitalist society the more the production of material wealth increases, the greater becomes the material inequality of the people. In this society the rich people recklessly squander colossal amounts of wealth on an utterly worthless, extravagant and dissolute life, but the poor people live in misery and abject poverty. In capitalist society many people are forced to lead an inhuman existence; they are compelled to sell even their human dignity and conscience in order to earn a living. In the final analysis, in capitalist society neither the rich nor the poor can be genuine masters of a sound material life.[1]

- In [a] capitalist society, the ideological and cultural life of the people is also very poor. There, the people have their independent thinking paralyzed and are degenerating ideologically and culturally because they are poisoned by the reactionary bourgeois ideology and culture. Even in what they call the most developed capitalist countries, the number of illiterate and mentally deformed people is ever increasing, and many people are degenerating into vulgar beings who seek only momentary comfort and pleasure without having any ideals or ambitions.[2]

■ In a capitalist society, the working masses cannot enjoy the cultural and emotional life in the true sense of the word. It is a reactionary society in which a handful of capitalists and other privileged classes violate the independence of the masses and oppress and exploit them. It is a rotten and degenerate society that is exclusively based on egotism and in which fraudulence and trickery, immorality and depravity, and decadent culture are rampant; a society ruled by the law of jungle. The exploiting class, for their own rapacity, are perpetrating murder, extortion and all sorts of inhuman, uncivilized actions without hesitation, enjoying pleasure in such behavior. The working masses in a capitalist society are the objects of exploitation and oppression. They are not provided with even the basic conditions for human life. In such a reactionary capitalist society, in which the independence of the masses is infringed upon and a small minority of the exploiting class lords it over the society, the cultural and emotional life is inconceivable for the working people.[3]

■ Capitalist society is a corrupt society where the masses' independence is trampled upon and violated without mercy. In this society a variety of means that gnaw at people's minds and bodies cut a wide swathe, reducing them to mental and physical cripples. As social evils of every description are ruling the roost, people full of terror and discomfort feel ill at ease. It is a reactionary society where a handful of landowners and capitalists live well-off, whereas the broad sections of the masses go poorly clothed and hungry, "the rich get richer" and "the poor get poorer." For the handful of the exploiting class, including the landowners and capitalist, capitalist society is a "heaven," whereas it is a hell for the absolute majority of the popular masses.[4]

■ To establish a revolutionary world outlook means that one equips oneself with the concept of transforming the old society; in other words, one arms oneself with the revolutionary idea and the viewpoint of destroying the exploitative society together with the classes that rule that society, in order to build socialism and communism. One also makes a firm decision to fight to the last for the victorious cause of socialism and communism. It is not a simple matter to establish a revolutionary world outlook. Such an outlook is not established in a few days with a few classes of instruction; it is formed, made firm and developed through certain developmental stages of consciousness. As the great leader has explained, the first stage of the formation of a revolutionary world outlook is to understand the essence of social phenomenon. In a society of hostile classes, the revolutionary consciousness of people begins to develop with a recognition of the irrationality of the exploitative society. Only when they correctly recognize the essence of capitalist society can they hate the landlords, capitalist class and exploiting society and acquire the determination to smash the class enemies and construct a new society free from exploitation and oppression. Beginning with their recognition of how landlords exploit peasants and how capitalist grind down workers in an exploiting society, people gradually become fully aware of the fact that the capitalist society in which money is almighty is the root of all human misfortune and misery and that this society is a reactionary one, hampering social progress.[5]

- To become a revolutionary, one must hate the exploiting class and society, become determined to overthrow the unreasonable social system and to devote oneself to the struggle for the construction of a new society—a socialist and communist society free from any exploitation and oppression. This is the third stage of the formation of a revolutionary world outlook.[6]

From Kim Jong-il's Talk to the Senior Officials of the Central Committee of the Workers' Party of Korea, titled, "Let Us March Forward Dynamically Along the Road of Socialism and Communism under the Unfurled Banner of the Anti-Imperialist Struggle," September 25, 1987

- The crisis of capitalism finds clear expression in the fact that the position of the United States, the ringleader of world imperialism, is becoming more and more difficult.

  The United States is in this difficult position because it is not only sharing the same crisis as the capitalist powers, but has also been gradually losing its leading position in the capitalist world. As their economic domination is being weakened as a result of the economic progress of the European capitalist countries and Japan, the U.S. imperialists are basing their economy more and more on armaments in order to maintain their domination over the capitalist world and allow the large munitions monopolies to make profits. As a result, the deficit in their state budget has become enormous, and their foreign debts have swollen so that the United States, which was once the greatest creditor country in the world, has, now, become the largest debtor nation.

Since in the United States the armaments monopolies are trying to make greater profits by ceaselessly expanding the munitions industry, the process of basing the economy on armaments cannot be halted. The United States has attended the negotiations on nuclear arms reduction, but in no way does this mean that its monopolies have abandoned their desire to expand the munitions industry. The American armaments monopolies may not regard the reduction of those nuclear weapons which have already been manufactured and sold as affecting their interests directly, but on no account will they tolerate any reduction or banning of nuclear arms production. That is why the United States, while negotiating for nuclear arms reduction, continues to push forward the adventurous "Star Wars" program, which is said to cost thousands of billions of dollars. It can never free itself from the heavy burden of its ever-growing military expenditure, and its budget deficit and foreign debts will increase further. In the long run, this will lead its economy into a bottomless mire.

■ Contemporary imperialism has also a serious inner contradiction because of which it cannot escape its doom.

Outwardly, the developed countries seem to be prospering, but inwardly they are rotting due to ever-worsening contradictions.

As the marketing channels are clogged to a greater extent, capitalists are moving towards deforming the material life of people by creating an artificial inhuman demand. They are manufacturing a variety of things to stimulate extravagance, corruption and dissipation and to paralyze the human body and mind, with the result that the number of drug addicts, alcoholics, as well as degenerates pursuing abnormal desires, is growing rapidly and people are becoming mentally and physically deformed. Even the defenders of the bourgeoisie are lamenting and calling this phenomenon an incurable disease of modern capitalism. The capitalists are frenziedly spreading reactionary and anti-popular ideas and culture, as well as the decadent bourgeois way of life, in order to paralyze the working masses' consciousness of independence and to make people submit to the capitalist exploiting system. In capitalist countries all manner of reactionary ideology and superstition which, like a narcotic, numb the sound mind of the people and make them ignorant, are widespread. The way of life in which the weak fall prey to the strong is fostered and, as a result, such social evils as immorality and depravity, murder and robbery arc rampant and people are trembling with fear and apprehension. Thus in capitalist society the mental life of the people becomes all the more intolerable with the increase in material wealth.

■ The U.S. imperialists and the international reactionaries are concentrating the spearhead of their attack on the socialist countries, which are the bulwark of peace and progress, and are brazenly attempting to stamp out the struggle of the progressive people of the world who desire independence. As the leader has said, the imperialists are now dancing around wielding a nuclear weapon in one hand and a purse in the other. The schemes of the imperialists are becoming ever more vicious and crafty as they try to bring the people of the socialist countries and other progressive people throughout the world to their knees by threatening and blackmailing them militarily, bribing and subordinating them economically and disrupting them ideologically and culturally.

Whenever imperialism faces a crisis, its reactionary and aggressive nature increases and it makes desperate efforts to maintain its existence. The frenzied efforts of the imperialists are not an expression of their strength; they reveal their vulnerability. The more reactionary the imperialists become and the more frenzied are the efforts they make, the more the people will be awakened to revolutionary awareness, and the day of the collapse of imperialism will draw nearer. It is an indisputable fact that the end of contemporary imperialism is nigh, and it is historically inevitable that imperialism will perish and socialism triumph.[7]

ELEVEN

Fidel Castro's Cuba

Fidel Castro is fading. He has been Cuba's dictator for almost fifty years, and in that time has served as a mouthpiece for every bit of anti-American propaganda. His Cuba is one of the most brutal dictatorships on the face of the earth. I have interviewed victims who have been imprisoned for crimes such as lending books to other Cubans and then brutalized in prison beyond our imagination.

Castro has also done his best to assist terrorists, from the Irish Republican Army to his own band of "revolutionaries" who—when the Soviet Union bankrolled them—fomented violent revolution all over Central and South America. Like Kim Jong-Il, Castro is best described by his own words. And, like his protégé and new bankroller Venezuelan Hugo Chavez, Castro's words appear in such great number—his speeches going on for hour after hour—it's necessary to excerpt them.

From the past to the present, a Fidel collage:[1]

1958

- When this war is over a much wider and bigger war will commence for me: the war I am going to wage against them [the United States]. I am aware that this is my true destiny.
- We accuse the U.S. government...of selling to the Batista dictatorship the planes and bombs that have killed so many defenseless Cuban civilians. If the U.S. violates our sovereignty we will defend it with dignity....We are ready to die in defense of our people.

1959

- If the Americans don't like what is happening in Cuba, they can land the Marines and then there will be 200,000 gringos dead.

1960

- If Kennedy were not an illiterate and ignorant millionaire, he would understand that it is not possible to carry out a [counter-] revolution supported by landowners against the peasants in the mountains, and that every time imperialism has tried to encourage counterrevolutionary groups, the peasant militia has captured them....Let no one think, however, that these opinions as regards Kennedy's statements indicate that we feel any sympathy toward the other one, Mr. Nixon, who has made similar statements. As far as we are concerned, both [Kennedy and Nixon] lack political brains.

1961

- The invaders [at the Bay of Pigs] came to fight for free enterprise! Imagine, at this time for some idiot to come here to say that he fought for free enterprise!

  A revolution expressing the will of the people is an election every day, not every four years; it is a constant meeting with the people.

  The people know that the Revolution expressed their will; the Revolution does not come to power with Yankee arms. It comes to power through the will of the people fighting against Yankee arms.

  If Mr. Kennedy does not like socialism, well, we do not like imperialism! We do not like capitalism! We have as much right to protest over the existence of an imperialist-capitalist regime ninety miles away from our coast as he feels he has to protest over the existence of a socialist regime ninety miles from his coast.

  Mr. Kennedy... does not have a clear concept of international law or sovereignty. Who had such notions before Kennedy? Hitler and Mussolini!

- I am a Marxist-Leninist and I shall be a Marxist-Leninist to the end of my life.

1962

- The duty of every revolutionary is to make the revolution. It is known that the revolution will triumph in America and throughout the world, but it is not for revolutionaries to sit in the doorways of their houses waiting for the corpse of imperialism to pass by. The role of Job doesn't suit a revolutionary. Each year that the liberation of America is speeded up will mean the lives of millions of children saved, millions of intelligences saved for culture, an infinite quantity of pain spared the people. Even if the Yankee imperialists prepare a bloody drama for America, they will not succeed in crushing the peoples' struggles, they will only arouse universal hatred against themselves. And such a drama will also mark the death of their greedy and carnivorous system.

At [the] Punta del Este [inter-American conference in Uruguay in 1961] a great ideological battle unfolded between the Cuban Revolution and Yankee imperialism. Who did they represent there, for whom did each speak? Cuba represented the people; the United States represented the monopolies. Cuba spoke for America's exploited masses; the United States for the exploiting, oligarchical, and imperialist interests; Cuba for sovereignty; the United States for intervention; Cuba for the nationalization of foreign enterprises; the United States for new investments of foreign capital. Cuba for culture; the United States for ignorance. Cuba for agrarian reform; the United States for great landed estates. Cuba for the industrialization of America; the United States for underdevelopment... Cuba for peace among peoples; the United States for aggression and war. Cuba for socialism; the United States for capitalism....

■ [The Soviet Union] could have installed a thousand [nuclear] missiles [in Cuba in 1962]! That's what I said to Biriouzov [the Soviet field marshal in charge of nuclear forces in Cuba]: a thousand missiles. I said to him: "Look, if it is in the interest and the defense of the entire socialist camp, we are prepared to install a thousand [nuclear] missiles here." Imagine my reaction when they told me that they would [only] install [40] missiles....

We defended these [nuclear] missiles with affection, with an incredible love. We were fighting for the first time almost on equal terms with an enemy [the United States] that had threatened and provoked us unceasingly.

I wrote a letter [on October 26, 1962] to Khrushchev to give him courage. It was my opinion that, in case of an invasion, it was necessary to launch a massive and total nuclear strike [against the United States].... If they invade...one should not waste time...nor give the enemy the time to launch the first strike.

1966

■ Between 1970 and 1980 Yankee imperialism will not have one square inch of imperialist property left in Latin America. We are absolutely certain of this.

Mr. Johnson, that big ignorant Texas cowboy, said recently that...revolutions are retreating, and he cited such cases as Indonesia and Ghana, and he mentioned several other countries.

[Yet] Vietnam is the place where Yankee imperialism, with all its criminal, reactionary, and savage spirit, is being disrobed. The U.S. attack on Vietnam cannot be compared with any other deed in contemporary history.

It is compared with Hitler's attacks on Poland and other small nations. However, the comparison cannot be made, because the crimes of the Yankees in Vietnam are worse than those of the German Nazis and the Italian Fascists, because of its [the United States] war resources, because of its destruction potential which is greater than that of the Germans and Italians, because of a similar lack of scruples. The Fascists never used toxic gases in the war. The United States uses not only conventional weapons in Vietnam, but also outlawed weapons like toxic gases, including bacteriological warfare. The only thing the United States has not used in Vietnam is the atomic weapon.

The hate which the imperialists have stirred up is such, the indignation which they have provoked throughout the world and in this part of the world—in our country—is such that we feel sure that there will not be a single combat unit of our armed forces which is not ready to be among the first ones to go fight the imperialist Yankees there [in Vietnam].

We know the imperialists. They love their skin too much. The imperialists are so cowardly—how many blackmailers! As long as they can wage a war without the least possible casualties, industrial losses, as long as they can pick the mangos from the low branches, as long as they can use their big power in increasing degree against a small country, they gain courage from it. But we know the imperialists very well—Johnson and his herd of outlaws: the Rusks, the McNamaras and their gang—who have been trapped in a dead-end street.

1967

- The problems of Yankee imperialism do not consist simply of finding ways to crush the Cuban revolution, but rather how to prevent the revolutionary throughout the continent from crushing Yankee imperialism.

■ To those who believe that peaceful transition [to communism] is possible in some countries of this continent, we say to them that we cannot understand what kind of peaceful transition they refer to, unless it is a peaceful transition in agreement with imperialism.

And those who believe that they are going to win against the imperialists in elections are just plain naïve; and those who believe that the day will come when they will take over through elections are super-naïve.

They'll never see... the Revolution hesitating, the Revolution giving up; they'll never see the Revolution yielding one iota of its principles! For Patria o Muerte [homeland or death] has many meanings. It means being revolutionaries until death, it means being a proud people until death! And the fact that we speak about Patria o Muerte does not mean that we have a sense of fatalism. It is an expression of determination. When we say "death," we mean that not only we would be dead, but many of our enemies would be dead, as well.

1978

■ Even though we don't like to be the ones to speak of the irreproachable way in which the Cuban revolution has fulfilled its internationalist duty, it should be recalled that our military cooperation with Angola and Ethiopia was not something new. Cuban soldiers went to the sister republic of Algeria in 1963 to support it against foreign aggression when, in the months following the victory of it heroic struggle for independence, attempts were made to a grab a part of its territory. Cuban soldiers went to Syria in 1973 when that country requested our help right after the last war waged against the Zionist aggressors. Cuban fighters fought and died to help free Guinea-Bissau and Angola from Portuguese colonialism. It is no secret that worthy comrades from our guerrilla struggle in the Sierra Maestra died with Che in Bolivia.

1999

- The United States of America...is involved [in Serbia] in what can be described, whether they like it or not, as genocide. [Cuba] cannot be conquered by anyone; no one can conquer a country that is willing to fight. It is wrong to try to conquer it. It already happened in Vietnam where the Americans understood it only when they had lost over 50 thousand lives and killed 4 million Vietnamese. Well, now, they are in a similar situation there, and one that can become more complicated if the Serbians everywhere give their support to the Serbians inside Serbia.

2000

- We are not ready for reconciliation with the United States, and I will not reconcile myself with the imperialist system. But if the American people and their government are ready to respect the rights of others, we are ready, in this case, to work so that peace prevails. Otherwise, there will be no reconciliation.

For the past forty years I have been struggling against the world's most powerful and dangerous force, and against the continuous embargo. Communist rule is still valid for the future because it is the most equitable system. We are defending our culture better than any other country because other countries are being subjected to a Western cultural invasion.

2001

- A new administration has just assumed power in the United States, in a rather irregular fashion. Everything known about the background and thinking of the main figures in this administration, the public statements made by many of them, before and after the highly unusual electoral process in which the Cuban-American terrorist mob played a decisive role in the questionable victory of the current president, has created an atmosphere of doubt, distrust and fear reaching practically all of the world public opinion.

- Forty years have passed [since the Bay of Pigs invasion]. Nevertheless, the methods of lies and deception used by the empire and its mercenary allies remain unchanged. When we see that south of the Rio Grande there is a whole collection of balkanized countries...about to be devoured by the mighty, expansionist and insatiable superpower of the turbulent and brutal north that scorns us, we Cubans can cry to the top of our voices: Bless the day, a thousand times over, that we proclaimed our revolution to be socialist! Without socialism, Cuba would not be the only country in the world today that does not need to trade with the United States in order to survive, and even to advance, both economically and socially.

Without socialism, Cuba would not have been able to endure the hostility of nine U.S. presidents.... I would have to add the one [George W. Bush] who has just assumed the presidential throne, since judging from his first steps in the international arena and the language of his advisors and allies in the Miami terrorist mob, there are signs that we could be facing a particularly aggressive and utterly unethical administration. At this very moment in history, the nations of Latin America are about to be devoured by the United States, the hegemonic superpower of today's world."

■ **The people and the governments of Cuba and Iran can bring the United States to its knees.** The U.S. regime is very weak, and we are witnessing this weakness from close up.

■ Women are accorded better treatment in some Islamic nations than in the West. In the West, women are regarded as a commodity and an object of business. I think of Western women as those who have been asphyxiated because of the way they're treated.

■ On Thursday [September 20, 2001], before the United States Congress, the idea was designed of a world military dictatorship under the exclusive rule of force, irrespective of any international laws or institutions. The United Nations, simply ignored in the present crisis, would fail to have any authority or prerogative whatsoever. There would be only one boss, only one judge, and only one law. We have all been ordered to ally either with the United States government or with terrorism. [Americans'] capacity to destroy and kill is enormous, but their traits of equanimity, serenity, reflection and caution are, on the other hand, minimal.

2002

■ Our heroes [five Cuban spies tried, convicted, and sentenced in 2001 for espionage against U.S. military installations] will have to be freed. The enormous injustice committed against them will be known by the whole world....

The U.S. government will never have the moral authority to combat terrorism while it continues to use such practices against nations like Cuba and to support massive, repugnant, and brutal massacres like those carried out by its ally Israel against the Palestinian people. With unparalleled arrogance and prepotency, it has threatened over eighty countries and taken the liberty of deciding which is a terrorist nation and which is not. It has even been so cynical as to include Cuba among the so-called terrorist nations, when thousands of Cubans have died as victims of terrorism perpetrated from the United States, while not a single American has ever suffered so much as a scratch, nor has the least of damage ever been caused by any such actions on the part of Cuba.

■ The power and prerogative of that country's [the U.S.] president are so extensive, and the economic, technological, and military power network in that nation is so pervasive that due to circumstances that fully escape the American people, the world is coming under the rule of Nazi concepts and methods.

Last September 20, 2001, when Mr. [George] W. Bush proclaimed [his war against terrorism]... at the same time, based on his military power he was assuming the role of world master and policeman. Long before the terrorist attacks of September 11, Bush had promoted enormous budgets for the research and production of more deadly and sophisticated weapons, although the Cold War was over....

[Bush perceives us as] the miserable insects that live in sixty or more countries of the world (chosen by him and his closest assistants)—and in the case of Cuba by his Miami friends—[which] are completely irrelevant. [We] are the "dark corners of the world" that may become targets of their unannounced and "preemptive" attacks.

What is the difference between that philosophy and methods and those of the Nazis? Why is it that so many governments are trembling with fear and keeping silent?

■ Arrogance, demagogy and lies are usually an inseparable part of [the U.S. president].

Mr. President, you are losing authority. In theory, you are empowered to bring death to a large part of the world, but you can't do it alone. You need many other people to help you obliterate the rest of the world and among the military and civilian leaders who operate in your country's power structures there are many learned and talented people...[who] will be less and less willing to be persuaded as they see that your political advisors lacking in capacity and military experience make one mistake after another. Dreadful and opportunistic lies do not suffice to launch preemptive and surprise attacks against any of the sixty or more countries [where terror cells are present, in reference to President Bush's speech at West Point on June 1, 2002], or against several of them, or against them all.

■ Hardly twelve years ago, many in the world expected to see Cuba, the last socialist state in the West, crumble. Not much time has gone by and today, instead, quite a number of us on this earth are waiting to see how the developed capitalist world led by the United States disengages from the colossal and chaotic economic mess in which it is enmeshed. Those who yesterday talked so much about the end of history might be wondering if this profound crisis is not the beginning of the end of the political, economic and social system it represents.

Perhaps, of the evils brought about by developed capitalism none is so nefarious as the way of life and the consumerist habits.

The set of problems that are piling up in the world point objectively to a disaster for neoliberal globalization and for that unsustainable economic order.

The smallest municipality in Cuba is stronger than all the scum that met with [President George W.] Bush in the James L. Knight Center in Miami.

2003

■ [Americans] say the world is moving towards democracy because the Chinese introduced some reforms. The Chinese have a political system very similar to Cuba's. They admit capitalists into the [Communist] Party. Our Party admits farmers earning a lot of money and religious people. . . . Bush could just as well say that, based on what we've done here in Cuba, that we're moving towards democracy.

We don't want to become a consumer society. . . . We have implemented a number of reforms but we're not headed towards capitalism. . . . We are not marching towards capitalism.

[We will not] change [Cuba's] constitution . . . [Cuba's] political system . . . [or Cuba's] economic system . . . in order to improve relations with the U.S.

We need to be cautious [about importing agricultural products from the U.S.] because we cannot be tied to only one source of supplies. It would be too risky so we continue purchasing commodities from our traditional suppliers.

Yes, my brother [Raúl Castro, the designated successor] has seniority but we should talk about the next generation. Even my brother is not that young. . . . I am thinking about the younger generation and how they are prepared to preserve the future. . . .

When Castro dies, what will replace him? Or will Cuba become a Venezuelan colony?

TWELVE

Hugo Chavez: Castro on Steroids

It seems the fate of all people who live in oil-rich nations—all people except Americans, that is—to be governed by dictators and despots, rogues and terrorists. Like Kim Jong-il, Venezuela's Hugo Chavez would be a comic book character were it not for his capabilities. Chavez is using Venezuela's oil to prop up Castro and propel Venezuela onto the world scene as a major player. For the good of his people? Judge for yourself.

On July 31, 2006, Chavez was in Tehran to accept the highest state award from his new Iranian pal, Mahmoud Ahmadinejad. This is the Associated Press report of the event:

Iran awarded Venezuelan president Hugo Chavez its highest state medal on Sunday for supporting Tehran in its nuclear standoff with the international community, while Chavez urged the world to rise up and defeat the U.S., state-run media in both countries reported.

The leftist Venezuelan leader also condemned Israel for what he called the "terrorism" and "madness" of its attacks in Lebanon, Venezuelan state television reported.

"Let's save the human race, **let's finish off the U.S. empire**," Chavez said. "This (task) must be assumed with strength by the majority of the peoples of the world."[1]

Two years earlier, the United States objected to Venezuela purchasing 100,000 Russian AK-47 assault rifles. In 2005, Chavez said the purchase was, "an honorable answer to President Bush's intention of being the master of the world."[2] (He has since obtained Russian agreement to build an AK-47 factory in Venezuela.)

In an August 2005 interview with al Jazeera, Chavez said: "What can we do regarding the imperialist power of the United States? We have no choice but to unite.... We will use oil in our war against neoliberalism."

In the same interview, according to one report, Chavez mocked Secretary of State Condoleezza Rice, "... whom he refers to as 'Condolencia,' which means 'condolence' in Spanish. In speeches, he has called her 'pathetic' and illiterate and made oblique sexual references to her. 'I cannot marry Condolencia, because I am much too busy,' he said in a recent speech. 'I have been told that she dreams about me,' he said on another occasion."[3] Chavez has also been quoted as saying, "The U.S. administration is behind the opposition in Venezuela, and Mr. George Bush has a black hat, black horse, and black flag. He is the main instigator and the main planner of all the movements that have attacked us."[4] As for his views on capitalism, Chavez has said, "I am convinced that the way to build a new and better world is not capitalism. Capitalism leads us straight to hell."[5]

But Chavez saved his strongest words for delivery at the UN. This is the text of his September 20, 2006, speech to the UN General Assembly:

Madam President, Excellencies, Heads of State, Heads of Governments, and high-ranking government representatives from around the world. A very good day to you all. First of all, with much respect, I would like to invite all of those, who have not had a chance, to read this book that we have read: Noam Chomsky, one of the most prestigious intellectuals of America and the world. One of Chomsky's most recent works: *Hegemony or Survival? America's Quest for Global Dominance*. An excellent piece to help us understand what happened in the world during the twentieth century, what is going on now and the greatest threat looming over our planet: the hegemonic pretension of U.S. Imperialism that puts at risk the very survival of the human species. We continue to warn about this danger and call on the people of the U.S. and the world to halt this threat, which is like a sword hanging over our heads.

I had considered reading from this book, but for the sake of time, I should just leave it as a recommendation. It reads easily; it's a very good book. I'm sure, Madam, you are familiar with it. It is published in English, German, Russian, and Arabic (applause).

I think that the first people who should read this book are our brothers and sisters in the United States because their threat is in their own house. The devil is right at home. The devil—the devil himself is right in the house.

And the devil came here yesterday. (Laughter.) Yesterday the devil came here, right here. (Laughter.) Right here. And it smells of sulfur still today.

This table that I am now standing in front of, yesterday, ladies and gentlemen, from this rostrum, the president of the United States, the gentleman to whom I refer as the devil, came here, talking as if he owned the world,

truly as the owner of the world. I think we could call a psychiatrist to analyze yesterday's statement made by the president of the United States.

As the spokesman of imperialism, he came to share his nostrums, to try to preserve the current pattern of domination, exploitation and pillage of the peoples of the world. An Alfred Hitchcok movie could use it as a scenario. I would even propose a title: "The Devil's Recipe."

As Chomsky says here clearly and in depth, the American empire is doing all it can to consolidate its hegemonistic system of domination, and we cannot allow them to do that. We cannot allow world dictatorship to be consolidated.

The world tyrant's statement—cynical, hypocritical, full of this imperial hypocrisy from the need they have to control everything—they say they want to impose a democratic model, but that's their democratic model. It's the false democracy of elites, and I would say a very original democracy that's imposed by weapons and bombs and firing weapons. What a strange democracy. Aristotle might not recognize it, or others who are at the root of democracy. What type of democracy do you impose with marines and bombs....

The president of the United States yesterday said to us right here in this room, and I'm quoting, "Anywhere you look, you hear extremists telling you you can escape from poverty and recover your dignity through violence, terror and martyrdom." Wherever he looks, he sees extremists. And you, my brother, he looks at your color and he says, oh, there's an extremist.

Evo Morales, the worthy president of Bolivia, looks like an extremist to him. The imperialists see extremists everywhere. It's not that we are extremists; it's that the world is waking up. It's waking up all over, and people are standing up. I have the feeling, dear world dictator, that you are going to live the rest of your days as a nightmare because the rest of us are standing up, all those of us who are rising up against American imperialism, who are shouting for equality, for respect for the sovereignty of nations. Yes, you can call us extremists, but we are rising up against the empire, against the model of domination.

The president then—and this he said himself—he said I have come to speak directly to the populations in the Middle East to tell them that my country wants peace. That's true. If we walk in the streets of the Bronx, if we walk around New York, Washington, San Diego, in any city—San Antonio, San Francisco—and we ask individuals, the citizens of the United States, what does this country want—does it want peace—they'll say yes. **But the government doesn't want peace. The government of the United States doesn't want peace; it wants to exploit its system of exploitation, of pillage, of hegemony through war.**

It wants peace, but what's happening in Iraq? What happened in Lebanon, Palestine? What's happening? What's happened over the last hundred years in Latin America and in the world, and now threatening Venezuela, new threats against Venezuela, against Iran? He spoke to the people of Lebanon. Many of you, he said, have seen how your homes and communities were caught in the crossfire. How cynical can you get? What a capacity to lie, shamefacedly. The bombs in Beruit, with millimetric precision, this is crossfire? He's thinking of a Western, when people would shoot from the hip and somebody would be caught in the crossfire. This is an imperialist fire, fascist, assassin, genocidal, the empire and Israel firing on the people of Palestine and Lebanon. That is what happened. And now we hear we're suffering because we see the homes destroyed.

The president of the United States came to talk to the peoples, to the peoples of the world. He came to say—I brought some documents with me because this morning I was reading some statements, and I see that he talked to the people of Afghanistan, the people of Lebanon, the people of Iran, and he addressed all these peoples directly. And you can wonder, just as the president of the United States addresses those peoples of the world, what would those peoples of the world tell him if they were given the floor? What would they have to say?

And I think I have some inkling of what the peoples of the south, the oppressed peoples think. They would say, "Yankee imperialist, go home!" I think that is what those people would say if they were given the microphone and if they could speak with one voice to the American imperialists.

And that is why, Madam President, my colleagues, my friends, last year we came here to this same hall, as we have been doing for the past eight years, and we said something that has now been confirmed fully, fully confirmed. I don't think anybody in this room could defend the system.

Let's accept; let's be honest: the UN system born after the Second World War collapsed. It's worthless. Oh yes, it's good to bring us together once a year, see each other, make statements and prepare all kinds of long documents and listen to good speeches like Evo's yesterday or President Lula's. Yes, it's good for that, and there are a lot of speeches and we've heard lots from the president of Sri Lanka, for instance, and the president of Chile. But we, the assembly, have been turned into a merely deliberative organ. We have no power, no power to make any impact on the terrible situation in the world.

And that is why Venezuela once again proposes here today, 20 September, that we re-establish the United Nations. Last year,

Madam, we made four modest proposals that we felt to be cru-
cially important. We have to assume this responsibility, our heads
of state, our ambassadors, our representatives, and we have to discuss these.

The first is expansion, and Lula talked about this yesterday
right here, the Security Council, both as regards permanent and
non- permanent categories. New developing countries and LDCs
must be given access as new permanent members. That's step
one.

Second, effective methods to address and resolve world conflicts. Transparent debates, transparent decision-making.

Point three, the immediate suppression—and that is something everyone's calling for—of the anti-democratic mechanism
known as the veto, the veto on decisions in the Security Council.

Let me give you a recent example. The immoral veto of the
United States allowed the Israelis with impunity to destroy
Lebanon, right in front of all of us as we stood there watching. A
resolution in the council was prevented.

Fourthly, we have to strengthen, as we've always said, the role,
the powers of the secretary-general of the United Nations. Yesterday the secretary-general practically gave us a speech of farewell,
and he recognized that over the last ten years things have just got-
ten more complicated—hunger, poverty, violence, human rights
violations have just worsened. That is the tremendous consequence of the collapse of the United Nations system and American hegemonistic pretensions.

Madam, Venezuela a few years ago decided to wage this battle
within the United Nations by recognizing the United Nations as
members of it that we are and lending it our voice, our thinking.
Our voice is an independent voice to represent the dignity and the
search for peace and the reformulation of the international system,

to denounce persecution and aggression of hegemonistic forces in the planet. This is how Venezuela has presented itself. Bolivar's home has sought a non-permanent seat on the Security Council. Let's see. Well, there has been an open attack by the U.S. government, an immoral attack, to try and prevent Venezuela from being freely elected to a post in the Security Council.

The imperium is afraid of truth, is afraid of independent voices. It calls us extremists, but they are the extremists. And I would like to thank all the countries that have kindly announced their support for Venezuela, even though the ballot is a secret one and there's no need to announce things.

But since the imperium has attacked openly, this strengthened the convictions of many countries and their support strengthens us. Mercosur as a bloc has expressed its support. Our brothers in Mercosur—Venezuela with Brazil, Argentina, Paraguay, Uruguay, is a full member of Mercosur—and many other Latin American countries—CARICOM, Bolivia—have expressed their support for Venezuela. The Arab League—the full Arab League has voiced its support. And I am immensely grateful to the Arab world, to our Arab brothers, our Caribbean brothers. The African Union, almost all of Africa has expressed its support for Venezuela, and countries such as Russia or China, and many others.

I thank you all warmly on behalf of Venezuela, on behalf of our people, and on behalf of the truth because Venezuela, with a seat on the Security Council, will be expressing not only Venezuela's thoughts, but it will also be the voice of all the peoples of the world, and we will defend dignity and truth.

Over and above all of this, Madam President, I think there are reasons to be optimistic. A poet would have said hopelessly optimistic because over and above the wars and the bombs and the aggressive and the preventive war and the destruction of entire peoples, one can see that a new era is dawning. As Silvio Rodriguez says, "the era is giving birth to a heart." There are alternative ways of thinking. There are young people who think differently, and this has already been seen within the space of a mere decade. It was shown that the end of history was a totally false assumption, and the same was shown about Pax Americana and the establishment of the capitalist neo-liberal world. It has been shown, this system, to generate mere poverty. Who believes in it now?

What we now have to do is define the future of the world. Dawn is breaking out all over. You can see it in Africa and Europe and Latin America and Oceania. I want to emphasize that optimistic vision.

We have to strengthen ourselves, our will to do battle, our awareness. We have to build a new and better world.

Venezuela joins that struggle, and that's why we are threatened. The U.S. has already planned, financed, and set in motion a coup in Venezuela, and it continues to support coup attempts in Venezuela and elsewhere. President Michelle Bachelet reminded us just a moment ago the horrendous assassination of the former foreign minister, Orlando Letelier.

And I would just add one thing. Those who perpetrated this crime are free, and that other event where an American citizen also died were American themselves—they were CIA killers, terrorists. And we must recall in this room that in just a few days there will be another anniversary. Thirty years will have passed from this other horrendous terrorist attack on the Cuban plane, where seventy-three innocents died, a "Cubana de Aviacion" airliner.

And where is the biggest terrorist of this continent, who took the responsibility for blowing up the plane? He spent a few years in jail in Venezuela. Thanks to CIA and then-government officials, he was allowed to escape, and he lives here in this country, protected by the government. And he was convicted. He has confessed to his crime. But the U.S. government has double standards; it protects terrorism when it wants to. And this is to say that Venezuela is fully committed to combating terrorism and violence, and we are one of the peoples who are fighting for peace.

Luis Posada Carriles is the name of that terrorist who is protected here. And other tremendously corrupt people who escaped from Venezuela are also living here under protection: a group that bombed various embassies, that assassinated people. During the coup they kidnapped me and they were going to kill me, but I think God reached down and our people came out into the streets and the army was true. And so I'm here today. But these people who led that coup are here today in this country, protected by the American government. And I accuse the American government of protecting terrorists and of having a completely cynical discourse.

We mentioned Cuba. Yes, we were just there a few days ago. We just came from there, happily. And there you see another era born. The summit of the fifteen, the summit of the Non-Aligned adopted a historic resolution. This is the outcome document. Don't worry, I'm not going to read it. But you have a whole set of resolutions here that were adopted after open debate in a transparent manner. More than fifty heads of state. Havana was the capital of the south for a few weeks, and we have now launched once again the group of the Non-Aligned with a new momentum. And is there anything I could ask all of you here—my companions, my brothers and sisters—it is to please lend your goodwill, to lend momentum to the Non-Aligned Movement for the birth of the new era to prevent hegemony and to prevent further advances of imperialism.

And as you know, Fidel Castro is the president of the Non-Aligned for the next three years, and we can trust him to lead the charge very efficiently if, unfortunately—they thought, oh, Fidel was going to die, but they're going to be disappointed because he didn't. And he's not only alive, he's back in his green fatigues and he's now presiding the Non-Aligned.

So, my dear colleagues, Madam President, a new, strong movement has been born, a movement of the south. We are men and women of the south.

With this document, with these ideas, with these criticisms, I'm now closing my file. I'm taking the book with me. And don't forget, I'm recommending it very warmly and very humbly to all of you.

We want ideas to save our planet, to save the planet from the imperialist threat. And hopefully, in this very century, in not too long a time, we will see this, we will see this new era, and for our children and our grandchildren, a world of peace based on the fundamental principles of the United Nations. But the renewed—a renewed United Nations.

And maybe we have to change location. Maybe we have to put the United Nations somewhere else, maybe a city of the south. We've proposed Venezuela.

You know that my personal doctor had to stay in the plane. The chief of security had to be left in the locked plane. Neither of these gentlemen was allowed to arrive and attend of the UN meeting. This is another abuse and another abuse of power on the part of the devil.

It smells of sulfur here, but God is with us and I embrace you all. May God bless us all. Good day to you. (Applause.)[6]

Conclusion

If man has a "natural" state, it is not a state of grace but a state of war. From the time of the Punic Wars between Rome and Carthage—which lasted 118 years from 264 to 146 B.C.—to the present day, men and nations have slaughtered each other with ever-increasing efficiency. The war in which America is now engaged may continue as long as the Punic Wars because Republicans (who call it the global war on terror) and Democrats (who don't admit it's a war at all) cannot agree on who the enemy is or how and where he should be fought. They cannot even agree on how victory can be defined, so they cannot chart a course to it.

Americans also remain confidently deluded about the reasons that wars begin. Too many of us believe that wars begin by mistakes that are usually avoidable. But history teaches us otherwise. Wars—big wars—begin because one nation believes that war is more advantageous than peace, and thus plans and commences hostilities. Wars are most often intentional acts that can be distinguished mostly by the care with which they are planned and carried out.

Because wars are intentional and not accidental, an enemy's intent must be derived from his intentions and his capabilities. When an enemy hides his intentions, they may still be deduced from his capabilities and those he seeks to build. But in our world—the world of the Internet and 24/7 news coverage, the ego-building lure of the camera, the need to recruit fanatic adherents to suicidal terrorism—creates a motherload of information that is there to be mined by each of us. Our enemies, and potential enemies, are advertising themselves almost every day. It is our job to listen and judge which are threats and which are blowhards.

My great friend, Ambassador Jose Sorzano, served as deputy to Jeane Kirkpatrick at the UN during the Reagan administration. He scoffs at those who speak ill of America, often reminding me of Cervantes' words, "Ladran señal de que cavalgamos," meaning "the dogs bark because we gallop." The little dogs, who speak ill of America only to gain attention and political influence among the other little dogs, are not the threat we face. But the global din they create is a fog that conceals the people and nations that do threaten us now, and will soon in the future.

The September 11 attacks proved that we cannot rely on our government—or the media—to do that for us. Each of us has the responsibility to listen, to evaluate, and to judge. The Internet—and invaluable resources such as MEMRI—give us a greater opportunity to read the words of our enemies and potential enemies than we have ever had in our history. To fail to do so is to fail in one of the most basic duties of citizenship.

We cannot know how many wars can be avoided if we listen to our adversaries, take them at their word, and assert our own interests—as we are entitled to do. The number of lives saved will be countless. To demand answers to those questions is a foolish diversion.

By their nature, politicians—both in Congress and the Executive Branch—are mostly unconcerned with anything that doesn't confront them on the front page of the newspaper or the first segment of the evening news. Just as the stock market drives companies to produce quarterly earnings rather than invest in the future, politicians are driven by poll numbers.

This unfortunate reality poses an overriding question we must all face: who among those who seek our votes can be trusted to not just listen but to absorb, analyze, and act? Which of the candidates even sees the need to do so? Politicians deliver what their constituents demand. If we ask too little of them, that is what we will receive.

Acknowledgments

My thanks are due first to Michelle Oddis for her dedicated and tireless research and to the Middle East Media Research Institute (MEMRI)—Yigal Carmon and the staff—whose extraordinary work made this book possible, and without which it could not have been done. To my friends Marji Ross, publisher, and Harry Crocker, chief editor and evil genius, my thanks for your help and your faith in my abilities (which often exceeds my talents). To my editors, Miriam Moore and Kate Frantz, my thanks for your calm and comprehensive efforts. And, as always, my love and thanks to my wife, Sharon, whose patience with my writing habits is above and beyond the call of wifely duty.

Appendix

Lieutenant Colonel Buzz Patterson was the Air Force officer assigned to carry the nuclear "football" for President Clinton. (The "football" is a briefcase with the codes and secure phone necessary for a president to launch a nuclear attack. The officer who carries it is the president's constant companion.) What happened when the CIA had located bin Laden and he was targeted for assassination? Here's Lieutenant Colonel Patterson's account from his book Dereliction of Duty:

THE WHITE HOUSE SITUATION ROOM was buzzing. It was fall 1998 and the National Security Council (NSC) and the "intelligence community" were tracking the whereabouts of Osama bin Laden, the shadowy mastermind of terrorist attacks on American targets overseas. "They've successfully triangulated his location," yelled a "Sit Room" watch stander. "We've got him."

Beneath the West Wing of the White House, behind a vaulted steel door, the Sit Room staff sprang into action. The watch officer notified National Security Advisor Sandy Berger, "Sir, we've located bin Laden. We have a two-hour window to strike." Characteristic of the Clinton administration, the weapons of choice would be Tomahawk missiles. No clandestine "snatch" by our Special Operations Forces. No penetrating bombers or high-speed fighter aircraft flown by our Air Force and Navy forces. No risk of losing American lives.

Berger ambled down the stairwell and entered the Sit Room. He picked up the phone at one of the busy controller consoles and called the president. Amazingly, President Clinton was not available. Berger tried again and again. Bin Laden was within striking distance. The window of opportunity was closing fast. The plan of attack was set and the Tomahawk crews were ready. For about an hour Berger couldn't get the commander in chief on the line. Though the president was always accompanied by military aides and the Secret Service, he was somehow unavailable.

Berger stalked the Sit Room, anxious and impatient. Finally, the president accepted Berger's call. There was discussion, there were pauses—and no decision. The president wanted to talk with his secretaries of defense and state. He wanted to study the issue further. Berger was forced to wait. The clock was ticking. The president eventually called back. He was still indecisive. He wanted more discussion. Berger alternated between phone calls and watching the clock. The NSC watch officer was convinced we had the right target. The intelligence sources were conclusive. The president, however, wanted a guaranteed hit or nothing at all.

This time, it was nothing at all. We didn't pull the trigger. We "studied" the issue until it was too late—the window of opportunity closed. Al Qaeda's spiritual and organizational leader slipped through the noose.

Notes

Introduction:

1. Winston Churchill writing of the period 1931–1935 in *The Gathering Storm*, 1948, 77–78.

Chapter One: Before September 11

1. "Bin Laden's Fatwa," OnLine NewsHour, PBS. Http://www.pbs.org/newshour/terrorism/international/fatwa_1996.html.
2. "CNN March 1997 Interview with Osama bin Laden," FindLaw.com. Http://fl1.findlaw.com/news.findlaw.com/hdocs/docs/binladen/binladen-intvw-cnn.pdf.
3. "Interview: Osama bin Laden," *Frontline*, PBS, May 1998. Http://www.pbs.org/wgbh/pages/frontline/shows/binladen/who/interview.html
4. Raphael Patei, *The Arab Mind*. (Long Island City: Hatherleigh Press, 2002), 332.
5. "Conversation with Terror," *Time*, January 11, 1999. Http://www.time.com/time/magazine/article/0,9171,989958,00.html.

Chapter Two: The Hate Factories

1. "Interview with the Hamas Leader," MEMRI Special Dispatch Series No. 3, July 30, 1998. Http://memri.org/bin/articles.cgi?Page=subjects&Area=jihad&ID=SP0398. The Hamas leader is Sheikh Ahmed Yassin and the interview was printed in *Al-Quds* on July 26, 1998.

2. "Friday Sermon on PA TV: Calling for Suicide Bombings," MEMRI Special Dispatch Series, June 12, 2001. No.228. Http://memri.org/bin/articles.cgi?Page=subjects&Area=jihad&ID=SP22801.

3. Palestine Television" [PA], June 8, 2001. Http://memri.org/bin/articles.cgi?Page=archives&Area=sr&ID=SR01002

4. "A Palestinian Weekly Raises Threats to Target American Embassies and Military Vessels," MEMRI Special Dispatch Series No. 264, , August 30, 2001. Http://memri.org/bin/articles.cgi?Page=subjects&Area=middleeast&ID=SP26401.

5. "Terror in America (30) Retrospective: A bin Laden Special on Al-Jazeera Two Months Before September 11," MEMRI Special Dispatch Series No. 319, December 21, 2001. Http://memri.org/bin/articles.cgi?Page=archives&Area=sd&ID=SP31901.

6. "Friday Sermons in Saudi Mosques: Review and Analysis," MEMRI Special Report No. 10, September 26, 2002. Http://memri.org/bin/articles.cgi?Page=archives&Area=sr&ID=SR01002.

7. John Bagot Glubb, *War in the Desert*, London, UK:(Houder and Stoughton, 1960), 47.

8. Dore Gold, *Hatred's Kingdom*, (Washington, D.C.: Regnery Publishing, 2003), 101.

Chapter Three: The Hate Networks

1. "President Discusses Global War on Terror," Press Release, White House Press Office, September 5, 2006. Http://www.whitehouse.gov/news/releases/2006/09/20060905-4.html.

2. "Al Qaeda Training Manual," United States Department of Justice web site. Http://www.usdoj.gov/ag/manualpart1_1.pdf.

3. Danielle Pletka, "Why the American Reluctance?" The American Enterprise Institute, Short Publications, December 22, 2005. Http://www.aei.org/publications/filter.all,pubID.23622/pub_detail.asp.

4. "'Why We Fight America:' Al-Qaida Spokesman Explains September 11 and Declares Intentions to Kill 4 Million Americans with Weapons of Mass Destruction," MEMRI Special Dispatch Series No. 388, June 12, 2002. Http://memri.org/bin/articles.cgi?Page=subjects&Area=middleeast&ID=SP38802.

5. Ibid.

6. Ibid.

7. Ibid.

8. "PA TV Broadcasts Call for Killing Jews and Americans," MEMRI Special Dispatch Series No. 138, October 13, 2000. Http://memri.org/bin/articles.cgi?Page=archives&Area=sd&ID=SP13800.

Chapter Four: The Hate Networks Aim at Iraq

1. "Abu Omar Al-Baghdadi: 'We Find No [Blood] Sweeter Than That of the Byzantines [i.e. Christians],'" MEMRI Special Dispatch Series No. 1454, February 7, 2007. Http://memri.org/bin/articles.cgi?Page=subjects&Area=jihad&ID=SP145407.

2. "Islamist Video Shows Preparation, Execution of Suicide Attack in Mosul," MEMRI Special Dispatch Series No. 1500, March 13, 2007. Http://memri.org/bin/articles.cgi?Page=subjects&Area=iwmp&ID=SP150007.

3. "ISI Spokesman: Only by Rolling Skulls and Spilling Blood Will We Achieve Victory," MEMRI Special Dispatch Series No. 1500, March 13, 2007. Http://memri.org/bin/articles.cgi?Page=subjects&Area=iwmp&ID=SP150007.

4. "Iraqi Militant Group 'The Arrows of God' Threatens to Kill Two German Hostages If Germany Does Not Withdraw Its Troops From Afghanistan Within Ten Days," MEMRI Special Dispatch Series No. 1500, March 13, 2007. Http://memri.org/bin/articles.cgi?Page=subjects&Area=iwmp&ID=SP150007.

5. "Mujahideen Issue a Video Ultimatum to Germany and Austria to Withdraw Their Troops from Afghanistan," MEMRI Special Dispatch Series No. 1500, March 13, 2007. Http://memri.org/bin/articles.cgi?Page=subjects&Area=iwmp&ID=SP150007.

6. Mariam Karouny, "Al-Zarqawi Killed in Joint Air Strike," Geelong Advertiser (Australia), June 9, 2006.

7. "Al-Qaida Leader Rebukes Muslim Clerics," WorldNetDaily, January 7, 2004. Http://www.worldnetdaily.com/news/article.asp?ARTICLE_ID=36483.

8. "A Documentary and a Discussion about Abu Mus'ab Al-Zarqawi," MEMRI TV Monitor Project, clip no. 391, November 28, 2004. Http://www.memritv.org/Transcript.asp?P1=391.

9. "Leader of Al-Qaeda in Iraq Al-Zarqawi Declares 'Total War' on Shi'ites, States that the Sunni Women of Tel'afar Had Their Wombs Filled with the Sperm of the Crusaders,'" MEMRI Special Dispatch

Series No. 987, September 16, 2005. Http://memri.org/bin/articles. cgi?Page=archives&Area=sd&ID=SP98705.

10. "Al-Qaeda Internet News Broadcast Celebrates U.S. Hurricanes and Gaza Pullout, Reports Zarqawi's Anti-Shiite Campaign and Chemical Mortar Shells in Iraq," MEMRI TV Monitor Project, September 2005. Http://www.memritv.org/Transcript.asp?P1=862.

11. "President Discusses Global War on Terror," White House Press Release, September 5, 2006. Http://www.whitehouse.gov/news/releases/2006/09/20060905-4.html.

12. "MEMRI TV Project: Saudi IQRA TV Examines Public Attitudes Toward Jews," MEMRI Special Dispatch Series No. 791, September 29, 2004. Http://memri.org/bin/articles.cgi?Page=archives&Area=sd&ID=SP79104.

13. "Prof. Nizar Riyan of the Hamas Political Leadership: Our Martyrs Are in Heaven, Their Dead Are in Hell," MEMRI TV Monitor Project, Clip No. 295, October 14, 2004. Http://www.memritv.org/Transcript.asp?P1=295.

14. "Three Years Later – The Arab and Iranian Media Commemorate 9/11," MEMRI Special Report No. 33, September 9, 2004. Http://memri.org/bin/articles.cgi?Page=archives&Area=sr&ID=SR3304.

15. "Saudi Professor of Islamic Law on Saudi TV Exhorts Muslims to 'Positive Hatred' of Christians," MEMRI Special Dispatch Series No. 1069, January 11, 2006. Http://memri.org/bin/articles.cgi?Page=archives&Area=sd&ID=SP106906.

16. "Cleric Muhammad Hassan on the Heroes of Falluja and Suicide Children," MEMRI TV, Clip No. 358, November 15, 2004. Http://memritv.org/Search.asp?ACT=S9&P1=358.

17. "Saudi Cleric Aed Al-Qarni Speaking at the Saudi Counter-Terrorism Campaign: The Jews and the U.S. Are the Ones Using Terrorism," MEMRI TV, Clip No. 535, February 7, 2005. Http://memritv.org/search.asp?ACT=S9&P1=535.

18. "Egyptian Sheik: Allah Be Praised—World Trade Center Fell, Thousands Converted to Islam," MEMRI TV Monitor Project, Clip No. 600, March 2, 2005. Http://www.memritv.org/Transcript.asp?P1=600.

19. "The First Ones to Kill and Use Terrorism in the World Were the Jews," MEMRI Special Dispatch Series No. 886, March 30, 2005. Http://memri.org/bin/articles.cgi?Page=archives&Area=sd&ID=SP88605.

20. "Jordanian Professor Ghazi Rabab'a: Muslims Will Return to Cordoba and Granada (Spain)," Free Republic, June 15, 2005. Http://www. freerepublic.com/focus/f-news/1423494/posts.

21. "Saudi Cleric Muhammad Al-Munajjid: Allah Finished Off the Richter Scale in Revenge of Infidel Criminals," MEMRI Special Dispatch Series No. 842," January 7, 2005. Http://www.memri.org/bin/articles.cgi?Area=sd&ID=SP84205.

22. "Al Qaeda threatens more UK, U.S. attacks ," CNN.com, Augst 4, 2005. Http://www.cnn.com/2005/WORLD/meast/08/04/zawahiri.london/index.html.

23. "Letter from al-Zawahiri to al-Zarqawi ," Office of the Director of National Intelligence, October 11, 2005. Http://www.dni.gov/press_releases/letter_in_english.pdf.

24. " Captured Iraqi Terrorist 'Adnan Elias: We Beheaded a Policeman, Filled His Corpse with TNT, and Used It to Blow Up Others," MEMRI TV Monitor Project, April 21, 2005. Http://www.memritv.org/Transcript. asp?P1=650.

Chapter Five: Iran: The Central Terrorist Nation

1. "Former Iranian President Threatens Force Against US and Israel," MEMRI Special Dispatch Series No. 233, June 22, 2001. Http://memri. org/bin/articles.cgi?Page=subjects&Area=middleeast&ID=SP23301.

2. "Leader's Address to High School Students," News Site of the Institute for Preserving and Publishing Works by Ayatollah Seyyed Ali Khomeini, March 14, 2005. Http://www.Khomeini.ir/EN/Speech/detail. jsp?id=20050314A.

3. "Leader's Speech to Government Officials on the Eid-al-Fitr," News Site of the Institute for Preserving and Publishing Works by Ayatollah Seyyed Ali Khomeini, November 4, 2005. Http://www. Khomeini.ir/EN/Speech/detail.jsp?id=20051104A.

4. "Iranian Friday Sermons, 2004–2006," Death to America DVD, www.memritv.org.

5. Ibid.

6. "Secretary of Iranian Guardian Council Ayatollah Ahmad Jannati:I Spit in the Face of the West, which Has Made Homosexuality Official and Legal," MEMRI TV Monitor Project, February 17, 2006. Http:// www.memritv.org/Transcript.asp?P1=1045.

7. "Terror in London (9) - Ayatollah Ahmad Jannati in Tehran Friday Sermon: The English Government May Have Caused the London Bombings Like the U.S. Government May Have Caused 9/11," MEMRI TV Monitor Project, July 15, 2005. Http://www.memritv.org/Transcript.asp?P1=758.

8. "Iranian Friday Sermons, 2004-2006," Death to America DVD, www.memritv.org.

9. "Iranian President Mahmoud Ahmadinejad: 'We Will Soon Experience a World Without the United States and Zionism,'" Press Release, The White House, September 5, 2006. Http://www.whitehouse.gov/news/releases/2006/09/20060905-7.html.

10. "Fact Sheets: #41, Iranian President Mahmoud Ahmadinejad," Jewish Virtual Library, December 19, 2005. Http://www.jewishvirtuallibrary.org/jsource/talking/41_iranpres.html.

11. "Transcript: Iranian President's Speech Threatening Israel,"Iran Focus, October 28, 2005. Http://www.iranfocus.com/modules/news/article.php?storyid=4164.

12. "Polling Only Solution to Palestine Problem, President," GlobalSecurity.org, December 14, 2005. Http://www.globalsecurity.org/wmd/library/news/iran/2005/iran-051214-irna02.htm.

13. "President Ahmadinejad: 'Your Doomed Destiny Will Be Annihilation, Misfortune And Abjectness,'" Press Release, The White House , September 5, 2006. Http://www.whitehouse.gov/news/releases/2006/09/20060905-7.html.

14. "Iranian Leader: Holocaust a 'Myth,'" CNN.com, December 14, 2005. Http://www.cnn.com/2005/WORLD/meast/12/14/iran.israel/index.html.

15. Nasser Karimi, (AP) "Iran Blames Israel for Cartoons, Denmark Pulls Ambassadors from Three Countries," OhMyNews.com, February 12, 2006. Http://english.ohmynews.com/articleview/article_view.asp?no=273849&rel_no=1.

16. "Iranian Friday Sermons, 2004-2006," Death to America DVD, www.memritv.org.

17. Ibid.

18. "Iranian President Ahmadinejad: The West Should Pick Up the Zionist Regime 'By the Arms and Legs' and Remove It from the Region; UN Resolutions Are Illegitimate; America & England are Enemies of the Iranian Nation," MEMRI Special Dispatch Series No. 1337, October 27, 2006. Http://memri.org/bin/articles.cgi?Page=subjects&Area=jihad&ID=SP133706.

19. "Ayat. Kashani: U.S.' anti-Iran charges are bubbles on limpid water," Islamic Republic News Agency, June 16, 2006. Http://www.irna.ir/en/ news/view/line-24/0606166941155610.htm.

20. "Terror in London (6) - Tehran Sermon: The U.S. and Israel are the Father and Mother of Al Qaeda; The Preacher Condemns London Attacks and the Crowd Cheers 'Death to England,'" MEMRI TV Monitor Project, July 8, 2005. Http://www.memritv.org/Transcript.asp?P1=747.

21. "Iranian Friday Sermons, 2004–2006," Death to America DVD, www.memritv.org.

22. Ibid.

23. Ibid.

24. Ibid.

25. Ibid.

Chapter Six: The Taliban, Pakistan, and Southwest Asia

1. "Interview with Mullah Omar – Transcript," BBC News, November 15, 2001. Http://news.bbc.co.uk/2/hi/south_asia/1657368.stm.

2. Isambard Wilkinson"Musharraf U-turn on Taliban," Telegraph, October 3, 2006. Http://www.telegraph.co.uk/news/main.jhtml?xml=/news/ 2006/10/03/wpak03.xml.

3. Http://www.realclearpolitics.com/articles/2006/03/_fighting_ the_ideological_war.html, reprinted with permission of RealClearPolitics.com.

Chapter Seven: Radical Islam Aims at Turkey

1. "Anti-Americanism in the Turkish Media," MEMRI Special Dispatch Series No. 870, February 25, 2005. Http://memri.org/bin/articles. cgi?Page=subjects&Area=middleeast&ID=SP87005#_edn8.

2. Ibid.

3. Ibid.

Chapter Eight: China: The Emerging Enemy

1. David Wallechinsky, "The World's 10 Worst Dictators," parade.com, February 13, 2005. Http://www.parade.com/articles/editions/2005/ edition_02-13-2005/featured_0.

2. Liang and Xiangsui, Unrestricted Warfare, Peoples' Liberation Army, Beijing, 1999. Translated and republished in 2002 by Pan American Publishing Co., Panama City, Panama. All citations are to the 2002 translation.

3. Ibid., 197.

4. Ibid., 76.

5. Ibid., 95.

6. Ibid., 123.

7. "Annual Report to Congress: The Military Power of the People's Republic of China," Office of the Secretary of Defense, 2006, 36.

8. Alexandra Harney, Demetri Sevastopulo, and Edward Alden, "Top Chinese General Warns U.S. over Attack," Financial Times, July 14, 2005. Http://www.ft.com/cms/s/28cfe55a-f4a7-11d9-9dd1-00000e2511c8.html.

9. "Annual Report to Congress: Military Power of the People's Republic of China 2006," Global Security.org. Http://www.globalsecurity.org/military/library/report/2006/2006-prc-military-power.htm.

10. "Annual Report to Congress: The Military Power of the People's Republic of China," Office of the Secretary of Defense, 2006, 2. Http://stinet.dtic.mil/dticrev/PDFs/ADA449718.pdf.

11. Ibid.,10.

12. "Speech by H.E. Mr. Hu Jintao, Vice President of the People's Republic of China at Dinner Hosted by 8 U.S. Organizations," Embassy of the People's Republic of China in the United States of America web page, May 1, 2002. Http://www.china-embassy.org/eng/zt/hjtfm/t36335.htm.

13. Dana R.Dillon, "China Threatens U.S. Alliances," FOXNews.com, March 23, 2005. Http://72.14.205.104/search?q=cache:sxlCt20MxhkJ:www.foxnews.com/story/0,2933,151094,00.html 1 China 1 threatens& hl=en&ct=clnk&cd=1&gl=us.

14. Annual Report to Congress: The Military Power of the People's Republic of China," Office of the Secretary of Defense, 2006, 11. Http://stinet.dtic.mil/dticrev/PDFs/ADA449718.pdf.

15. "President Jiang Zemin Meets the New York Times," Embassy of the People's Republic of China in Canada, October 24, 2003. Http://ca.china-embassy.org/eng/xwdt/t37302.htm.

16. "Foreign Ministry Spokesperson's Press Conference on September 2, 2003," Ministry of Foreign Affairs of the People's Republic of China. Http://www.fmprc.gov.cn/eng/xwfw/2510/2511/t25603.htm.

17. "Missile Defense-Related Statements and Developments," Nuclear Threat Initiative, Database. Http://204.71.60.36/db/china/mdchr.htm.

18. Ibid.

19. "Statement by Chinese Foreign Ministry Opposing US Imposition of Missile Proliferation Sanctions," Nuclear Threat Initiative, Database, September 5, 2001. Http://www.nti.org/db/china/engdocs/fmresp.htm.

20. "National People's Congress Foreign Affairs Committee Issues Statement on the Military Actions Against Iraq by the United States and Other Countries," The Nuclear Threat Initiative, March 21, 2003. Http://www.nuclearthreatinitiative.org/db/china/engdocs/npciraq_032003.htm.

Chapter Nine: Putin's Russia

1. "President Bush and President Putin Talk to Crawford Students," Press Release, The White House Office of the Press Secretary, November 15, 2001. Http://www.whitehouse.gov/news/releases/2001/11/20011115-4.html.

2. "Interview with Arab Satellite Channel Al-Jazeera," President of Russia Official Web Portal, February 10, 2007. Http://www.kremlin.ru/eng/text/speeches/2007/02/10/2048_type82916_118122.shtml.

3. Speech and the Following Discussion at the Munich Conference on Security Policy," President of Russia Official Web Portal, February 10, 2007. Http://www.kremlin.ru/eng/speeches/2007/02/10/0138_type82912type82914type82917type84779_118135.shtml.

4. "Putin Rejects Bush's Iraq Democracy Model,"CNN.com, July 17, 2006. Http://www.cnn.com/2006/WORLD/europe/07/15/russia.g8/index.html.

5. "BBC Monitoring Quotes from Russian Press Tuesday 28 February 2006," BBC Monitoring International Reports, February 28, 2006.

6. Ibid.

7. Ibid.

8. Ibid.

9. Ibid.

10. Ibid.

11. Ibid.

12. Peter Finn, "Putin Says Russia, U.S. Differ on Hamas Win," *Washington Post*, February 1, 2006, A19. http://www.washingtonpost.com/wp-dyn/content/article/2006/01/31/AR2006013100700.html.

13. "Putin: Hamas Not a Terror Organization," YNetNews.com, February 9, 2006. Http://www.ynetnews.com/articles/0,7340,L-3213707,00.html.

14. "Answers to Questions from the Russian Media Following a Visit to the Middle East," President of Russia Official Web Portal, February 13, 2007. Http://www.kremlin.ru/eng/text/speeches/2007/02/13/1400_type82914type82915_118375.shtml.

Chapter Ten: Kim Jong-il's North Korea

1. Kim Jong-il, *Selected Works* 9, 272–273.
2. Ibid., 273.
3. Ibid., 283–284.
4. Ibid., 331.
5. Kim Jong-il, *Selected Works* 2, 42–43.
6. Ibid., 44.
7. "Kim Jong-il 1987 Speech to KWP Central Committee Officials," BBC Summary of World Broadcasts, The Far East Special Supplement, September 28, 1998.

Chapter Eleven: Fidel Castro's Cuba

1. All quotations take from: Hans de Salas-del Valle, ed., Fidel Castro on the United States, Selected Statements, 1958-2003, Institute for Cuban and Cuban-American Studies Occasional Paper Series, February 2003. Http://www6.miami.edu/iccas/FidelontheUS-Hans.pdf.

Chapter Twelve: Hugo Chavez: Castro on Steroids

1. Nasser Karimi, "Hugo Chavez Receives Iran's Highest Honor," Associated Press, July 30, 2006. Http://www.breitbart.com/article.php?id=D8J6NURG0&show_article=1.
2. Kevin Sullivan, "Chavez Casts Himself as the Anti-Bush," Washington Post, March 15, 2005, A01. Http://www.washingtonpost.com/wp-dyn/articles/A35193-2005Mar14.html.
3. Ibid.
4. Dale Hurd, "Hugo Chavez vs. America," CBN News. Http://www.cbn.com/cbnnews/news/050531a.aspx.

5. "A Black Hat, Black Horse, and Black Flag," National Post (Canada), August 25, 2005.

6. "Remarks by Hugo Chavez, President of Venezuela, at the 61st United Nations General Assembly," Federal News Service, September 20, 2006.

Index